Personnel Management and Productivity in City Government

Personnel Management and Productivity in City Government

Selma J. Mushkin
Frank H. Sandifer
Georgetown University

Lexington Books
D.C. Heath and Company
Lexington, Massachusetts
Toronto

54599

Library of Congress Cataloging in Publication Data

Mushkin, Selma J. 1913-
    Personnel management and productivity in city government.

    Bibliography: p. 171
    Includes index.
    1. Municipal government—United States. 2. Municipal officials and employees—United States. 3. Personnel management—United States. I. Sandifer, Frank H., joint author. II. Title.
JS356.M87   352'.005'10973   78-21196
ISBN 0-669-02805-3

Published simultaneously in Canada.

Printed in the United States of America.

International Standard Book Number: 0-669-02805-3

Library of Congress Catalog Card Number: 78-21196

Contents

List of Figures
and Tables

Figures

Tables

Preface

In 1975 and 1976, the National Science Foundation (NSF) awarded seven research grants through its RANN (Research Applied to National Needs) program for the study of productivity measurement in administrative services.[1] The program announcement noted the growth trend in administrative-managerial occupations in both public and private enterprise in the United States and further noted that very little productivity research had dealt with the administrative services in either business or government. The seven research grants were intended, therefore, as a first step in focusing needed research attention on administrative productivity.

This report on personnel management and productivity in city governments presents the results of one of the projects. The other six were:

1. Purchasing: Robert M. Monczka and Phillip L. Carter, Graduate School of Business Administration, Michigan State University.
2. Purchasing and materials management services: Francis E. Plonka, Wayne State University.
3. Computing and information services: H.D. Greenberg, Westinghouse R&D Center, C.H. Kriebel, Graduate School of Industrial Administration, Carnegie-Mellon University.
4. Computing and information services: William M. Morris and Scott Sink, Department of Industrial and Systems Engineering, Ohio State University.
5. Inspection and quality control administration: Everett E. Adam, Jr., Management Department, University of Missouri-Columbia, James C. Hershauer and William A. Ruch, College of Business Administration, Arizona State University.
6. Budget and management analysis: Peter Merrill, Abt Associates, Inc.

The original NSF project monitor for the seven projects was Dr. Richard Mason. However, Dr. Mason left NSF in 1976. Upon his departure, Mr. Nello Zuech became project monitor for the six projects just listed. The seventh, the Public Services Laboratory (PSL) project on personnel management, was separated from the others, and Dr. Neal Dumas became project monitor for it, a role assumed later by Dr. Vaughn Blankenship.

The method used by NSF in approaching the issue of administrative productivity was to focus on fairly limited, ostensibly discrete aspects of administration, as illustrated by the list of projects. The attempt was made to identify and concentrate on specific service functions within the administrative organization of either public or private institutions. Thus the subject of the PSL study, as originally identified in the NSF program announcement, was "personnel administration and training." However, one of the earliest conclusions reached in the PSL effort was that there was little to be gained—and much to be lost—from separating the service function of personnel administration from the rest of personnel management. Abt Associates reached a similar conclusion about their subject of study, budget and management analysis.[2]

Personnel management (the term we prefer), or personnel administration, is not a discrete administrative service, either in government or in business. It does include an administrative-service responsibility, in that part of what a central personnel office or agency does is to provide certain services to others in the organization. However, that service responsibility does not comprise the entirety of the personnel agency's activities and responsibilities, nor does the personnel agency itself represent anything like the totality of personnel management. To focus study exclusively on a limited part of personnel management would be akin to analyzing one position on a basketball team, without regard for the other four positions, the players, and the coach. We address the concept of personnel management throughout this book.

The NSF program announcement for this series of projects reflected two kinds of interest in administrative functions. First, there was a concern for the impact that the substantial growth in administrative-managerial employment had on overall productivity. Second, there was an interest in trying to assess the productivity of particular administrative workers. It was our view, and that of the cities' representatives to the project, that the former concern clearly was the more important. Thus the primary question was not how to measure the productivity of workers engaged in personnel activities; rather it was what impact personnel management has on employee productivity and governmental performance in cities.

In addition, we should point out that at about the time of this project, a sizable effort was in progress to design and demonstrate efficiency measures for personnel offices in the federal government.[3] It was our hope at the outset, and remains so, that our efforts and those of the federal interagency task force would be complementary.

PSL's proposal to NSF for the study of personnel management called for a two-staged effort. This book represents the conclusion of the first phase. In the final chapter of this book, we briefly outline what we and the other project participants believe is a much needed follow-on, or phase II, study effort.

One important part of our project-related activities that is not dealt with elsewhere in the book is the formal and informal sharing of ideas and information about personnel management and productivity. In March 1977 we began dissemination of a guidebook, called *Assessing Personnel Management: Objectives and Performance Indicators,*[4] which was a direct outgrowth of the project. We greatly appreciate the participation and co-sponsorship of the U.S. Conference of Mayors, National League of Cities, and International Personnel Management Association in the publication of the guidebook.

Our information-sharing efforts also involved participating, along with representatives of the eight-city group, in various conferences and meetings of government officials and professionals. We hope that through participation in such conferences we succeeded in disseminating some of the important ideas and results produced during the project and, more important, in encouraging others to get involved in assessing personnel management performance. Some of the groups that gave us the opportunity to participate and make presentations to their conferences and meetings were: IPMA Mount Vernon Chapter, IPMA International Conference, IPMA Philadelphia Area Chapter, Work In America Institute and Labor Management Relations Service (conference on productivity and work quality), National Association of Tax Administrators (annual meeting), ICMA annual conference, and NLC Congress of Cities. As a follow-on to the project and continuation of the information-sharing efforts, we developed and conducted a 1-day workshop on personnel management and productivity at the annual meeting of the American Society for Public Administration and participated in the western regional conference of IPMA.

This project would not have been possible without the support, cooperation, and participation of the eight project cities and their representatives, the U.S. Conference of Mayors, and the National League of Cities. We cannot express strongly enough our admiration and appreciation of the project working group, which included the following people: Dayton, Ohio: Mr. Len Roberts, Administrator, Office of Intergovernmental Affairs; Lakewood, Colorado: Mr. Bill Henderson, Assistant City Administrator; Nashville-Davidson, Tennessee: Mr. Elmer D. Young, Technology Agent, Office of the Mayor; Savannah, Georgia: Mr. Tim Witsman, Director of Management Services; St. Paul, Minnesota: Mr. Peter Hames, Office of the Mayor; Scottsdale, Arizona: Mr. Rodger Neve, Budget Officer (now Deputy City Manager, Gainesville, Florida); Tacoma, Washington: Mr. Erling O. Mork, City Manager, and Ms. Regina L. Glenn, Director, Technology Transfer Center (left Tacoma in 1977 to take a position with the State of Washington); Worcester, Massachusetts: Mr. Demitrios M. Moschos, Executive Assistant to City Manager; U.S. Conference of Mayors: Mr. Melvin A. Mister.

We also are indebted to John Gunther, Executive Director of the U.S. Conference of Mayors, for his support of the project. The members of the project advisory board, who are listed on page xiii, provided invaluable guidance and suggestions, especially concerning the specification of personnel management objectives and performance indicators, as did Charles Warren.

Our colleague at PSL, Douglas P. Wagner, was closely and valuably involved in the design, conduct, and analysis of the eight-city survey. Kenneth J. Coffey, formerly of PSL, was instrumental in getting the project underway. And Violet M. Gunther of PSL provided important assistance from beginning to end.

Other contributors to various stages of the project or part of this report are Charles Vehorn, Sally Familton, Frank Dehn, Lisa Hoffman, Lynn Norman, Kitty Conlon, Mahesh Sharma, Veronica Nieva, and Carol Edwards. We also want to thank Ann Guillot and Alva Wood for outstanding secretarial assistance and manuscript preparation.

Notes

1. National Science Foundation, *Research on Productivity Measurement Systems for Administrative Services*, NSF Program Announcement no. 75-14 (Washington, D.C.: National Science Foundation, Division of Advanced Productivity Research and Technology, 1975).

2. P. Merrill and J.K. Kumar, *Productivity Measurement in Administrative Services: Budgeting and Management Analysis in Public Service Institutions*, Report no. AAI-77-56 (Cambridge, Mass.: Abt Associates, June 1977).

3. J.D.R. Cole and A.S. Udler, "Productivity and Personnel," *Civil Service Journal* 17(2):23 (October-December 1976).

4. S.J. Mushkin, F.H. Sandifer, and C. Warren, *Assessing Personnel Management: Objectives and Performance Indicators* (Washington, D.C.: Public Services Laboratory, Georgetown University, March 1977).

Selma J. Mushkin
Frank H. Sandifer

Members of the Project Advisory Board

Wayne Anderson
Advisory Commission on Intergovernmental Relations

Enid Beaumont
International Personnel Management Association

Nancy Hayward
National Center for Productivity and Quality of Working Life

Donald S. Wasserman
American Federation of State, County and Municipal Employees

Mark Keane
International City Management Association

Keith Mulrooney
American Society for Public Administration

Joe Robertson
National Association of Schools of Public Affairs and Administration

David T. Stanley
Consultant, formerly with the Brookings Institution

Graham Watt
National Training and Development Service

Sam Zagoria
Labor Management Relations Service

1 Introduction

Setting the Stage

Administrative-management functions and services, especially in the cities, are being scrutinized today more carefully than ever before. There are many reasons for this deepened concern. For one thing, the familiar crusade against government inefficiency is being stepped up, against a backdrop of the fiscal squeeze of inflation and citizen resistance to tax increases. The public is demanding accountability, and programs are being assessed for benefits and costs, each balanced against the other. In some places, efforts at budget reform through zero-base budgeting give new emphasis to indepth program assessment. In many others, evaluations of existing programs intensify the search for ways to achieve greater efficiency and to reduce government's size and cost.

A major factor in the probe of administrative services in the cities is the current size of the federal financial commitment and the prospect of further enlargement of intergovernmental city aids that lies ahead as new national and state urban policies are formulated. Federal assistance now makes up 13 percent of the general revenues of the cities. Federal and state aids combined account for 40 cents of each dollar of city general revenue. The federal aids increased from 4 percent to the 13 percent figure in just a decade. Even in a single fiscal year, 1976, federal aids increased 27 percent, and the end is not in sight. When federal and state funds become as important as they are in city finances, it is inescapable that the tax-levying governments will seek to get the most for their investment. Assessment of "overhead" as administrative costs is a byproduct. The picture of the financial dependence of cities is sharpened when the interdependency is examined by city size (see table 1-1).

Over $26 billion, about 40 percent of city government general funds, go toward payroll. These outlays in wages and salaries paid to city officials and employees are exclusive of the city contributions for retirement, health insurance, and other fringe benefits. When the city contributions for retirement payments are added, the total is increased to $32 billion.

Any serious effort to increase the output per dollar of city governments must include an analysis of the relationship between personnel management and the effectiveness of city services. Certainly, the methods by which employees are selected, hired, managed, motivated, and rewarded determine, in large part, the impact and efficiency of any organization in serving its clients or constituents.

Table 1-1
Revenues in the Cities: 1975-76

	General Revenue (per capita)	Intergovernmental Revenue (per capita)	Intergovernmental as a Percent of Total Revenue	Own Revenue as a Percent of Intergovernmental Revenue	Property Taxes as a Percent of Total Revenue	Property Taxes as a Percent of Own Revenue	Own Revenue (per capita)	Property Taxes (per capita)
All cities	$405	$163	40%	148%	26%	43%	$242	$104
Cities of 100,000-500,000 population[a]	425	165	39	158	27	43	260	113
100,000-199,999	392	149	38	163	32	51	243	124
200,000-299,999	433	176	41	146	24	40	257	104
300,000-499,999	474	185	39	156	21	35	289	100
Average of the eight cities[b]	417	142	34	211	24	36	275	118
Dayton	404	125	31	223	12	17	279	48
Lakewood	127	28	22	357	9	12	100	12
Nashville-Davidson	625	207	33	202	33	49	419	204
St. Paul	394	148	38	166	31	50	246	122
Savannah	263	88	33	199	31	46	175	81
Scottsdale	292	116	40	153	14	23	177	40
Tacoma	408	135	33	202	11	17	273	46
Worcester	820	291	35	182	47	73	530	388

Source: U.S. Bureau of the Census, *City Government Finances in 1975-76*, Series GF76, No. 4, U.S. Government Printing Office, Washington, D.C., 1977.

[a]Weighted average.
[b]Unweighted average.

City administrators and elected officials are by no means the only ones subjected to increased public pressure for accountability. Public employee unions also have witnessed a deterioration of public sympathy for escalated salary and benefit demands. They, too, are coming under increasing fire from a more vocal citizenry which demands accountability, on one hand, and decries increased taxation, on the other. It can be of little surprise that both labor and management are currently seeking ways to improve the effectiveness and efficiency of city services.

Background

Personnel management in cities as an aspect of administrative services has been largely ignored in municipal research. Analysis of such management activities, accordingly, starts with an almost clean slate. What is being sought as an end product is a method of identifying the objectives and designing criteria for assessing the progress made toward those objectives, so that at a later phase optional processes may be formulated and examined to ascertain how best to achieve those objectives at lowest cost.

Even within the limited context of an explanatory analysis, there are serious obstacles to examination of personnel management. The specification of objectives of personnel management must be illustrative, except in the context of a particular government, by the officials of that government and for defined us s of that government. Designation of criteria to assess progress made by management processes is dependent on each government's formulation of those objectives in the aggregate and for personnel functions. Costing of alternative processes is handicapped by the lack of data. Budget information is at best incomplete. Furthermore, so little is known about the basic relationships between personnel management functions, processes, and their costs that development and testing of models of fixed and variable costs are also impaired. Far more than the numbers of public employees and their turnover rates must be known.

In response to the growing demand for research dealing with administrative services and productivity, a joint Public Services Laboratory/National League of Cities/U.S. Conference of Mayors study on personnel management was undertaken. Eight cities were selected by the Conference of Mayors for participation and study. Selection criteria included size, geographic location, experience in productivity measurement or improvement, and interest in participation. The following municipalities, scattered across the nation and of medium size (with populations between 75,000 and 450,000), were chosen: Dayton, Ohio; Lakewood, Colorado; Nashville-Davidson, Tennessee; St. Paul, Minnesota; Savannah, Georgia; Scottsdale, Arizona; Tacoma, Washington; and Worcester, Massachusetts.

Design of the Study

Convergence of the notions of productivity in government through improved personnel management and of personnel management as an integral component of government management is the core of the eight-city study. How might these notions be examined, given the diversity and pluralistic patterns characteristic of American cities?

For a better grasp of the problem, several factors that essentially determine developments in personnel management must be better understood:

The current formulation of objectives of personnel management (and changes required in those formulations) if productivity assessment is to be given a priority position

The types of criteria or measurements of progress toward the achievement of these defined objectives

The full range of costs of personnel management, including costs of inadequate or misguided management

The gains in overall accountability and services to the public that can be expected to follow on improved personnel management

The contribution of each of the components of personnel management to the achievement of gains in government effectiveness and quality of working life

The idea was to design a study that emphasizes the interrelations of (1) processes of personnel management as an integral part of city management and (2) personnel aspects of program effectiveness.

In inviting cities' participation in the study, John Gunther, Executive Director of the U.S. Conference of Mayors, wrote:

The project should produce results which will be beneficial to elected local officials in carrying out their responsibilities for making difficult policy decisions about service levels, budgets, and reorganization. The success of the project will depend in part on the involvement and participation of staff people in many different departments of city government. It is the linkage between effective provision of government services, personnel practices, budget procedures, and internal management of city government departments which is of importance to the project.

The study design in this respect was unusual. It was novel to call for top-level support that would permit personnel management to be assessed as a part of city management and city policy formulation *or* as an integral part of the political processes of responding to the public.

More recently, several additional actions have been taken to further encourage top elected and administrative officials in the cities to concern themselves with personnel management so that the vital tasks of guiding personnel, staffing services, and providing incentives for high-level performance are not kept separated from the rest of management.

For example, the International City Management Association (ICMA) and the International Personnel Management Association (IPMA) are involved in a joint effort under the heading of "Management Approaches to Personnel Problems." They are developing training modules and handbooks to help top local government administrators respond to some of their most difficult and time-consuming personnel problems.[1]

Involving the top leadership of the city in the effort was an essential step in the study design. But other decisions about study design were also important, including decisions on how many cities should be a part of the initial study. And which cities? These decisions placed in balance such elements as (1) the divergence of cities, or their uniqueness, so that some minimal number is required to gain perspective on current practices and prospects for changes; (2) the differences in function, for example, between central cities and suburban communities; (3) the variation in intensity and scope of expenditures between geographic regions, and (4) the structures of the cities, including political structures and management styles. Certainly, city size makes for much variation in scope, expenditures, and so forth. A small number of cities was chosen to permit adequate study and collaboration, and the selections were reduced to those between 75,000 and 500,000 in population, where the processes are not overwhelmed by bigness, yet are large enough to necessitate routinized personnel practices.

It was decided that eight cities would be an appropriate number for study. The issue of location also was resolved with due regard for "balance" but with special emphasis on geography, that is, representation of each of the major regions of the United States. Another very important consideration that guided the choices was experience and interest in productivity improvement and productivity-measurement application.

Given the purpose of studying productivity improvement in and by personnel management, it made good sense to focus the initial inquiry on city governments that had a background of productivity efforts. Studying cities that had taken steps to bring about more effective performance or improved staffing arrangements would permit researchers to draw on an existing body of experience and profit from the spade work done before.

The study's aim of disseminating findings and use of such dissemination as a catalytic agent for improving public personnel management generally gave added weight to the decision to work jointly with at least eight cities. This number probably is the smallest number that would provide leadership to encourage replication if replication were indicated and to yield data on the variety and range of experiences about steps toward change.

The Eight Cities in the Total of All Cities

The cities selected may be described in a variety of ways that place them in the context of cities generally. In the sections that follow, some selected characteristics of the eight cities are set forth for this purpose.

The eight cities run the gamut of economic circumstances. Two of the eight—Worcester, Massachusetts and Dayton, Ohio—are cities whose economies have been depressed and where unemployment in recent years has been relatively high. Nashville, Tennessee and Savannah, Georgia are enjoying the comparable prosperity of the Sun Belt area.

Growth rates (measured by per capita income increases 1959-1975) for standard metropolitan statistical areas (SMSAs) are shown in table 1-2. The SMSAs in which the eight cities are located, on the average, were growing at a somewhat more rapid annual rate than all economic regions—8.3 versus 7.7 percent. However, Worcester's growth over the period 1959-1975 was below average, and the Phoenix area (Scottsdale) was substantially above average (although in the year 1975-1976, Phoenix dropped to the bottom of the eight cities in per capita income growth).

While each of the eight cities is unique, on average they are not unrepresentative of the cities of the United States and those within a population size of 100,000 to 500,000. The mean general revenue per capita of the eight cities was $417 in 1975-1976 (as shown in table 1-1). For all cities, it was $405. General expenditures in the eight cities for noneducational services (table 1-3) ranged from $131 in Lakewood to $800 per capita in Worcester. For all cities in 1975-1976, it was $398 per capita. Police and fire expenditures averaged $70 per capita for the eight cities. For all cities, it was $68 per capita (table 1-3).

Table 1-2
Economic Growth of the SMSAs for the Eight Project Cities: 1959-1975

	Per Capita Personal Income				Increase per Annum		
	1959	1969	1974	1975	1959-1975	1969-1975	1974-1975
United States	$2,167	$3,733	$5,486	$5,903	7.70	8.96	8.46
Average of the eight SMSAs	2,173	3,795	5,517	5,950	8.32	9.04	9.01
Dayton	2,463	4,141	5,633	6,016	6.70	6.27	6.43
Denver-Boulder	2,510	3,920	6,096	6,641	9.18	11.77	9.32
Nashville	1,851	3,412	5,202	5,638	8.86	10.34	9.91
Phoenix	2,058	3,617	5,589	5,763	11.00	12.71	6.38
St. Paul-Minneapolis	2,472	4,288	6,078	6,533	7.95	8.15	7.89
Savannah	1,582	3,256	4,834	5,356	7.99	8.39	12.51
Tacoma	2,214	3,920	5,377	5,955	8.08	7.41	12.34
Worcester	2,231	3,808	5,327	5,695	6.78	7.33	7.27

Source: Bureau of Economic Analysis, U.S. Department of Commerce, *Survey of Current Business* 57(4), April 1977.

Table 1-3

Per Capita Expenditures of City Governments in the Eight Project Cities: Total and Selected Major Functions: 1976

	General Expenditures	Education	Police-Fire	Parks and Housing
All cities	$398	$ 56	$68	$30
Cities 100,000-500,000 population[a]	438	71	80	43
100,000-199,999	404	77	73	37
200,000-299,999	451	70	78	41
300,000-499,999	485	63	92	52
Average of the eight cities[b]	416	−	70	31
Dayton	427	−	96	77
Lakewood	131	−	36[c]	10[d]
Nashville-Davidson	623	249	66	17
St. Paul	388	7	75	49
Savannah	246	−	59	21[d]
Scottsdale	280	−	48	22
Tacoma	433	−	93	24
Worcester	800	295	88	30

Source: U.S. Bureau of the Census, *City Government Finances in 1975-76*, Series 6F76, No. 4, U.S. Government Printing Office, Washington, D.C., 1977.

[a]Weighted average.

[b]Unweighted average.

[c]Police only.

[d]Parks-recreation only.

The primary industrial composition of the SMSAs in which the eight cities are located is shown in table 1-4. Four of the eight cities are in SMSAs in which manufacturing and earnings employment is larger than average. In the Tacoma, Dayton, St. Paul, and Denver SMSAs, government is considerably larger than average. In Tacoma it is almost twice the average share.

The guide to productivity improvement projects developed by ICMA for the National Center for Productivity and Quality of Working Life was used in making the initial city selections. The types of efforts listed in the guide included projects that may be identified as management by objectives, program budgeting, development of measurement systems for performance, policy analysis and performance auditing, and the like.

The cities that were asked to participate in the study of personnel management by and large had much experience with a variety of types of productivity-improvement projects. Since the mid-1960s, Dayton and Nashville[2] have been participating in efforts to improve policy analysis, specify program objectives, and develop criteria for assessing progress toward the achievement of those objectives. Savannah also has a long history of similar effort on performance budgeting, needs assessment, and policy analysis. Scottsdale has had much

Table 1-4
Industrial Composition of Economic Areas Measured by Relative Earnings, by Industry: 1975

Economic Area	Manufacturing	Construction	Wholesale-Retail Trade	Finance, Insurance, and Real Estate	Transportation, Communications, and Public Utilities	Services	Government (Federal, State, and Local)
For all United States economic areas	19.3%	4.3%	12.7%	4.0%	5.4%	12.1%	13.8%
Average of the eight SMSAs	19.8	4.7	13.7	4.3	5.5	12.3	16.2
Dayton	30.8	3.5	11.8	2.5	3.4	11.3	19.3
Denver-Boulder	14.2	5.4	16.1	5.7	7.2	14.2	15.6
Nashville[a]	20.6	6.2	16.3	5.8	5.4	14.7	11.9
Phoenix	14.0	5.2	14.0	5.6	5.0	13.4	14.0
St. Paul-Minneapolis	22.4	4.5	16.6	5.2	7.1	12.7	11.8
Savannah	16.9	5.9	13.2	3.4	8.2	11.7	17.4
Tacoma	12.3	3.7	11.2	2.7	3.4	9.9	27.5
Worcester	27.2	2.8	10.1	3.3	3.9	10.1	12.0

Source: Regional Economics Information System, Bureau of Economic Analysis, U.S. Department of Commerce.

Note: Information is for SMSA.

[a]1974 data.

experience with innovative projects and is a city much concerned with technology application. Lakewood is essentially a new residential city designed from the outset as an innovative government, experimenting with new organizational structures and tools. Tacoma has become an important technology-transfer center, working with both the National Science Foundation and local industry to achieve improved application of technology to city government. Similarly, Worcester, Massachusetts and St. Paul, Minnesota have undertaken innovative efforts to improve services and lower costs. Worcester, for example, has established a steering committee to find executives in private industry who will, on a part-time basis, volunteer services to the city. It also has been using paraprofessionals to perform certain routine tasks in the police department as a way to release trained police officers for crime prevention and investigation. St. Paul has recently been involved in efforts to establish greater control and accountability, including revision of the form of government from commission (without chief executive) to strong mayor-council.

This quick description of productivity efforts in the eight cities is only suggestive. An understanding of the variety of sequences by which city governments over the years come to build a capacity for assessment of public services and the productivity of public servants is of great importance in moving from the particular cases of individual cities to broader dissemination in the interest of better city government.

Research Aims

Just exactly what was to be studied? The officials of the eight cities, drawing on their own priorities, emphasized the barriers to productivity improvement in the cities imposed by the routines of personnel administration. The productivity of personnel management itself initially was regarded as of lesser interest.

One consequence of this priority ranking was the two-part treatment of productivity and personnel management, with one part addressing perceptions of officials on personnel management functions and their impact on the implementation of productivity improvement efforts and the other the productivity of the personnel management processes.

Cost analysis as a central study topic was initially discussed but was postponed for subsequent study. Several considerations suggested this change. First, the formulation of concepts of cost components that had been expected to be carried out by others and to be available to the study project was not done. The basic conceptual work needed to make cost an operational study component would have had to become a part of the study project itself and require delays in other phases of the work. Clearly, understanding the size and number of the several offices of personnel in the cities was itself of some importance in underscoring the diversity of responsibility and the potential pulling and hauling among personnel staffs with different missions and different allegiances. However, the design of an accounts system that would permit the range of personnel management costs to be recorded would have added to the time required for the research and would have run the costs beyond the amount of the NSF grant. Again, the lack of prior study of cost analysis meant a new and major effort to fill the gap, which went beyond the potential scope of the immediate study.

Instead, the study focused on (1) experimentally formulating objectives of personnel management and its components, (2) developing illustrative criteria by which the major objectives of personnel management might be assessed, and (3) beginning an assessment of effectiveness criteria of personnel management by gathering views of officials in the eight-city survey on the relation of personnel management to productivity as the single most pervasive purpose of personnel management.

The chapters that follow have been organized to present the project's findings, conclusions, interpretations, and methodologies in a manner that we hope is both logical and informative. Chapter 2 describes and reports the results of our effort to achieve useful measures across cities of the perceived effects of personnel management on productivity. The survey that was designed and conducted as part of the project represented the primary thrust of our direct research within the eight city governments. Chapters 3 and 4 are intended to be companion pieces, the former dealing principally with the conceptual framework of examining personnel management performance (concentrating mostly on effectiveness) and the latter dealing with the costs of personnel management, including cost-analysis techniques and uses. In chapter 5 we have drawn together some of the results of other relevant research, the eight-city survey findings, and the practical wisdom of the city representatives and other practitioners in a summary discussion of ways that personnel management in the cities affects productivity. A particular aim of chapter 5 is to present significant observations and conclusions in a way that will be useful for local government elected officials, managers, and employees. Chapter 6 is a brief description of a plan of study for what we and the participating cities have concluded is a very significant and timely follow-on research effort. It focuses on the application of productivity measurement in personnel management as a part of the broader and apparently cumulative process of management change in city governments.

Appendix A presents additional details on the methodology and design of the eight-city survey, including a sample copy of the survey instrument. Appendix B describes results of the survey that are not discussed in chapter 2.

Notes

1. Some of the major problem areas to be addressed in the ICMA-IPMA work are: employee performance evaluation, women in management, the interface between personnel systems and general management, work planning, employee orientation, and employee-management relations.

2. The Metro Government of Nashville, of course, is itself innovative. It is the only consolidated city-county government among the eight project cities.

2 Personnel Management Performance in the Eight Cities

There are numerous problems and pitfalls in trying to assess the overall effectiveness of personnel management in municipal government. The process is even more difficult if one is seeking a measure of performance across several cities. Some practical method of achieving an assessment of personnel management performance in each of the eight cities is needed so that the results also can be aggregated for the cities as a group.

The survey that was designed and administered as part of this project represents our attempt to conduct a limited assessment of personnel management performance across the eight cities. The concern was focused on what may be called the first basic objective of personnel management: *to provide the human resources required for effective and efficient delivery of needed services to the public.*

An Overview of the Survey Results

Which components of personnel management appear generally to have a negative effect on productivity-improvement efforts in the cities? Which ones seem generally to help? These and similar questions were the focus of the participating cities' interest in the eight-city survey. Answers to them, except on a city-by-city basis, necessarily require enough consensus among the survey respondents to allow for broad generalizations. We were admittedly interested to see what degree of consensus would be found, given the considerable diversity of the cities and respondents.

In fact, very substantial consensus was found on a number of the survey questions. Because of that, we are able, in subsequent parts of this chapter, to discuss in some detail impediments, supports, and potential supports to the cities' productivity-related actions.

Analysis of the survey results shows that in general the following four broad personnel management components are most likely to be viewed as negatively affecting productivity actions: collective bargaining, compensation, promotions/transfers/terminations, and classification. Three others generally are perceived as supporting productivity actions: performance appraisal, employee development, and employee-employer relations. The EEO-Affirmative Action component is not generally seen as having a significant impact, either positive or negative. It is not possible to make a broad generalization about the remaining personnel management component, recruitment and selection.

The results of the eight-city survey are discussed in some detail in the remainder of this chapter, in chapter 5, and in appendix B. The discussions in this chapter are intended principally to report and provide some interpretation of the direct survey findings. In chapter 5, the survey results are mentioned in the context of a broader discussion of policy implications about productivity and personnel management.

Survey Design

The significant research question at the outset of the survey design effort was formulated as follows: How well does personnel management contribute to the effectiveness and efficiency of service delivery? As initially stated, this question contained two broad measurement issues:

How to measure effectiveness and efficiency of service delivery (and changes in effectiveness and efficiency)

How to measure personnel management's contribution to effectiveness and efficiency

The first of these issues was at least partly answered by the eight cities' representatives to the project at the first project meeting. Their unanimous concern focused on the barriers to productivity improvement created by the personnel management policies, rules, practices, and procedures in their cities. The eight cities involved are activist and innovative cities, they were selected for the project in part because of their records in productivity improvement. Part of what they wanted from this project was a systematic appraisal of where the problems are in personnel management—in a sense, a map of where personnel management potholes are on the road to greater effectiveness and efficiency for their operations.

Their comments provided us the opportunity to both respond to some of the cities' direct needs and resolve the issue of finding a measure of service-delivery effectiveness and efficiency. Thus we decided to reformulate the basic survey question to the following: What impact has personnel management had on productivity-improvement efforts? While not all the cities have established measurements of overall effectiveness and efficiency for their governments' services, each of them has undertaken numerous significant efforts to improve the effectiveness or efficiency of the government generally or of specific programs and services. Rather than using a generic term like productivity-improvement efforts, we defined this concept by the use of city-specific, productivity-related activities with which the managers and employees of the cities would be familiar. In essence, then, we used city-specific productivity actions to represent the concept of productivity improvement, which itself was a surrogate for the unavailable measures of overall effectiveness and efficiency of government service delivery. (Appendix 2A, at the end of this chapter, lists the productivity actions included in each city's surveys.)

The second issue—how to measure the impact of personnel management—presented additional problems. The greatest of these was simply the diversity among the cities in terms of their arrangements for personnel management. Some have civil service commission systems and others do not—Worcester, for example, comes under the state civil service system of the Commonwealth of Massachusetts. Some have very loosely structured personnel management systems, while others have very formalized systems. Some are moving in the direction of more centralized control of personnel management functions, while others are moving in the opposite direction. How to design a standard assessment technique that could successfully encompass all the variety was the challenge.

We ended up with a survey aimed at achieving a perceptional assessment of personnel management's impact in the eight cities. We asked management officials and employees of the cities for their observations on various aspects of personnel management in relation to the cities' productivity-improvement efforts. The key to accepting the value of this type of assessment is the recognition that if managers in a government perceive that a particular part of the personnel management system is a problem, then that perception itself represents a dysfunction of personnel management in the government.

In designing the survey instrument (questionnaire), we overcame the problem of diversity in personnel management among the eight cities by developing a listing of the major components of personnel management in any sizable government, regardless of the functional arrangements for implementing those components. Those components are as follows:

Recruitment and selection. All the activities starting with reaching potential job applicants and ending with appointment of new employees, including preparing and distributing recruiting materials, operating job information centers, advertising jobs, visiting schools and other sources of candidates, examining and rating applicants, certifying eligible candidates, selecting candidates, and appointment.

Classification. The system or process of evaluating jobs or positions and arranging them into occupational groups, classes, and grade levels on the basis of similarities of duties, responsibilities, and qualification requirements. A classification system may cover all city employees, or it may cover only certain segments of the employee population.

Compensation. The plan or system of providing equitable salaries (pay) and benefits for employees. Included are the statutory or regulatory bases for city salaries and benefits and such activities as salary comparability surveys, construction of multiranged pay plans, and cost-analysis of employee benefits (such as holidays and paid leave, health and life insurance, retirement, and the like)—all the functions which, taken together, make up the development, implementation, and maintenance of the total compensation system of the city.

Performance appraisal. The program or system for regular, periodic evaluations of employees' job performance. Some fairly common types of performance appraisal are production record reviews, supervisors' rating scales, field reviews or audits, critical incident appraisals, essay appraisals, self-evaluations, peer reviews, and subordinate appraisals.

Employee development. A program of, or provisions for, enhancing personal or career development through (1) training or instruction that is closely related to on-the-job application and is either provided or arranged by the city government and (2) other means such as short-term developmental assignments, planned increments of experience, and incentives for outside education (e.g., college or trade school programs), including approved absences from work and whole or partial tuition payments.

Promotions, transfers, and terminations. The separate but related processes of promoting, reassigning, and firing employees, each of which includes statutory and/or regulatory bases for the personnel action, the criteria for determining who and when (e.g., who may be promoted and when), and the actual decisions to effect the personnel action.

Employee-employer relations. The formal and informal exchanges of views and positions concerning productivity actions and program changes between management and employees. The consultations could involve individual employees as well as employee organizations and unions. The consultations could be either structured or unstructured and could take place from the initial planning phase for the productivity actions or program changes through the development, implementation, operation, and final critique.

Collective bargaining. All the activities within the city government related to obtaining and supporting the contracts or work agreements between the city and employee unions and organizations concerning the services of city employees. This includes such functions as conducting talks and formal negotiations of contracts with unions and/or employee organizations, handling day-to-day dealings with their representatives on contract issues, administration of the contracts, conducting research and staff support for the talks and formal negotiations, and administration of the formal grievance procedures.[1]

EEO-Affirmative Action. All the activities related to establishing and enforcing antidiscrimination policies, as well as establishing and implementing Affirmative Action guidelines or quotas.

Personnel staffing levels. The system or process of making major decisions on city program or department staffing levels.[2]

In each of the eight cities, PSL administered the survey instrument to a group of top government administrators, managers, and a few elected officials, all of whom were selected by the city's representative to the project in consultation with PSL project staff. Generally included were the chief administrative officer (mayor, city manager, or city administrator) and assistants, heads of major line departments, personnel director and professional staff, budget and/or finance officials and analysts, productivity or technology-transfer staff, and other high-level managerial employees who were chosen for their knowledge of productivity or human resource issues in the governments. The number of people surveyed varied from city to city, depending mainly on the size of the city and the organization of the government. This variation in the sample size was dealt with in the analysis by weighting the responses so that the results for each city count equally.[3]

A couple of additional points must be made about the survey's design and capabilities. First, the survey focused on fairly discrete areas within the personnel management framework of the cities generally but did not attempt to define specific conditions. In that sense, the survey focused on *where* (e.g., where the problems are, where the supports for productivity are) rather than on *what* (specifically what is the problem). Again, this aspect of the survey was dictated by the diversity among the cities in their personnel management arrangements. For example, if a majority of respondents across all cities indicated that "procedures for getting positions classified properly" impeded city productivity actions, that does not define precisely what procedures were perceived as impediments. Some respondents may have had in mind their cities' very detailed, cumbersome, and time-consuming classification procedures, while others were relating to the absence of any formal procedures in their governments. Second, the reported results focus primarily on respondents' consensus about the *direction* of the impact of personnel management factors, not the *degree* of such impact. (Appendix A presents additional details on the survey methodology and administration.)

Effects of Productivity Actions on City Services

The first question of the survey asked respondents to indicate what impact they believed the specific, listed productivity actions had had on the quality of their city's services. The survey was not aimed at evaluating the cities' productivity-improvement efforts. Rather, this question was intended to accomplish two purposes: (1) to induce the respondents to concentrate on the specific productivity actions that were listed rather than on some vague notion of productivity, and (2) to provide us some indication of whether the listed productivity actions had caused improvements in productivity or performance in city services. The productivity actions that were included in the questionnaires are described, by city, in Appendix 2A.

Across all eight cities, about 82 percent of respondents believed that the listed productivity actions had "helped" the quality of city services. There was, however, considerable variation between cities, as shown by table 2-1.

In one sense, the differences substantiate the validity of the survey, in that they show that the responses were *not* merely random marks on a page. However, interpretation of the differences is somewhat difficult. We tend to attribute the differences to three main factors:

1. *The choice of productivity actions.* City representatives and PSL staff used three basic criteria for selecting the specific productivity actions to be included in each city's survey. They were that the actions chosen should be (a) as familiar as possible to people throughout the government, which meant that they would be very broad, citywide or interdepartmental efforts if possible, (b) at a stage of implementation that the impact could be gauged, and (c) fairly recent, that is, implemented within the last two or three years. It was not always possible to fulfill these criteria, and some of the response differences undoubtedly result from this shortcoming. Also, not all the productivity actions selected for inclusion were intended to have a direct impact on the quality of services.

2. *Environmental/political variables.* There quite possibly is a "productivity publicity" variable that influenced the responses. Scottsdale and Lakewood, for example, have been hailed by various groups and organizations in recent years for their innovations and the impact of their productivity-improvement efforts. This type of publicity might have influenced the perceptions of the respondents. In addition, there is substantial difference among the cities

Table 2-1
Impact of Specific Productivity Actions on the Quality of City Services, Aggregated by City
(percentage distribution of responses)

City	Impeded	No Impact	Helped
Dayton	11.2%	11.2%	77.6%
Lakewood	3.4	5.7	90.8
Nashville	4.4	11.5	84.0
St. Paul	9.4	26.4	64.4
Savannah	0	21.7	78.4
Scottsdale	3.6	6.2	90.2
Tacoma	3.8	17.1	79.2
Worcester	1.5	20.0	78.5
Weighted average	6.0	12.2	81.8

in terms of the stated aims of the elected and appointed leadership. Improving the quality of services may be the central aim in some cities but may not be the major emphasis in others.

3. *The effects of the productivity actions on respondents.* We have noted earlier that the survey basically concentrated on high-level managers in each of the governments. We cannot avoid noting, also, that in some cities the respondents as a group were the people most likely to have been directly affected by some of the major productivity actions. Under Dayton's reorganization of city administration, for instance, a number of the managers surveyed formerly reported directly to the city manager but now report to assistant city managers. One would expect that the differential impacts of the productivity actions on the survey respondents would account for at least some of the variation in responses to this question.

Average Impact of Personnel Management Components

Following the introductory section of the questionnaire were nine sections, one about each of the personnel management components discussed earlier (excluding personnel staffing levels, as noted previously). The opening question in each of these sections asked respondents what impact they believed the broad personnel management component had had on implementation of each of the listed city productivity actions. The results are summarized in table 2-2.

On examining table 2-2, the first things one is likely to note are the large proportion of responses in the "no impact" column and the generally small

Table 2-2
Overall Impact of Nine Personnel Management Components on Eight Cities' Productivity Actions
(*average percentage distribution of responses*)

Personnel Management Component	Impeded	No Impact	Helped
Recruitment and selection	5.3%	51.2%	43.5%
Classification	14.1	53.1	32.8
Compensation	12.8	54.8	32.4
Performance appraisal	3.4	54.6	41.9
Employee development	2.3	41.5	56.2
Promotions, transfers, terminations	17.0	51.8	31.2
Employee-employer relations	15.4	41.5	43.1
Collective bargaining	19.3	65.3	15.4
EEO-Affirmative Action	8.7	74.8	16.5
Aggregate average	10.9	54.3	34.8

Note: The distributions reported in this table represent averages of respondents' ratings of the impact of nine broad personnel management components on the implementation of four to seven specific productivity actions in each city. Individual responses are weighted so that each city's responses count equally.

proportion in the "impeded" column. Some readers may want to take heart in these results—"See, personnel management isn't as bad as everyone claims." We do not necessarily disagree with the sentiment, but it is not supported by these results. In responding to a question about a broad subject (e.g., the recruitment and selection program in general), there is some tendency to answer "no impact" rather than to choose a positive or negative response.

Table 2-3 presents a different method of rating the various personnel management components. After the initial question in each section about the broad component, a list of significant elements or factors within that component was presented. Respondents were asked how each of those specific factors had affected implementation of their city's productivity actions. Table 2-3 is a broad summary of the results. We mentioned earlier the tendency of respondents to answer "no impact" to questions about broad or general subjects. This observation is confirmed by a comparison of tables 2-2 and 2-3. The latter was obtained by aggregating the responses to the separate factors in each personnel management component and then averaging them to achieve an overall average response for the component. There is much less concentration of responses in the "no impact" category (29.2 percent on average, compared with 54.3 percent in table 2-2).

The average distributions shown in table 2-3 clearly suggest some of the generalizations that were put forth earlier. For instance, 60.8 percent of the responses about factors in performance appraisal are in the "helped" category, compared with only 21.2 percent in "impeded." Similarly, 60.2 percent on employee development are in "helped," while 18.6 percent are in "impeded." On the other side of the response scale, 40.3 percent of the responses about collective bargaining factors are in "impeded," while only 22.6 percent are in "helped."

Table 2-3
Overall Impact of Personnel Management Components Based on Averaging Responses to the Factors within Each Component

	Impeded	No Impact	Helped
Recruitment and Selection	30.8%	27.4%	41.8%
Classification	34.6	24.5	40.9
Compensation	38.4	24.5	37.1
Performance appraisal	21.2	18.0	60.8
Employee development	18.6	21.3	60.2
Promotions, transfers, terminations	36.3	37.9	25.8
Employee-Employer relations	28.2	19.1	52.8
Collective bargaining	40.3	37.1	22.6
EEO-Affirmative Action	30.7	53.2	16.1
Average	31.0	29.2	39.8

Note: The distributions reported in this table represent the averages of respondents' ratings of the impact of the nine broad personnel management components on the implementation of four to seven specific productivity actions in each city. Individual responses are weighted so that each city's responses count equally.

In the following three sections, we group some of the most significant survey results into three categories: impediments, supports and potential supports.

The Impediments

The results of the survey questions about the specific elements or factors within each component of personnel management serve to highlight some of the most severe problem areas. Such is the case with the seven personnel management factors shown in table 2-4. Respondents clearly felt that these factors were barriers to their cities' productivity-improvement efforts. Out of a total of 45 personnel management factors listed in the nine sections of the questionnaire, these seven were most clearly perceived as impediments.

It is interesting to note that five of the seven factors concern procedures (although the performance rewards and terminating-for-cause factors combine both policies and procedures, making differentiation impossible). It is possible that some of the respondents answered these questions negatively out of frustration with procedures in general. However, we must note that the established procedures are an important part of all the personnel management functions, and that the respondents' opinions are not less significant just because they are addressing those procedures.

Table 2-4

Impediments: Aggregate Percentage Distribution of Responses to Seven Personnel Management Factors

	Impeded	No Impact	Helped
1. Procedures for getting positions classified properly	45.9%	17.3%	36.8%
2. Procedures for establishing or changing pay levels	48.2	18.1	33.7
3. Policies and procedures for rewarding superior performance (through increased pay or benefits)	43.5	28.7	27.8
4. Policies and procedures for terminating employees "for cause"	44.4	27.6	28.0
5. Procedures for processing promotion, transfer, and termination actions	39.8	29.5	30.6
6. Number of separate bargaining units (collective bargaining)	52.2	38.9	8.9
7. Attitude of unions or employee organizations toward productivity as a bargaining issue	60.8	27.8	11.4

Note: The distributions reported in this table represent the averages of respondents' ratings of the impact on productivity actions in general of four to seven specific factors within each personnel management component. Individual responses are weighted so that each city's responses count equally.

1. *Procedures for getting positions classified properly.* In most formal systems of personnel management, the classification program is the foundation for many of the other personnel management functions, such as recruiting, compensation, promotions and transfers, employee performance appraisal, and training. A breakdown in the classification process can have serious and far-reaching effects. Two possible reasons for the negative reactions of respondents might be the time delays that often occur in getting new positions classified and the frequent conflicts between managers and personnel specialists over who knows best how specific jobs should be classified.

2. *Procedures for establishing or changing pay levels.* Our observation, on talking with those surveyed and others in each of the cities, is that the area of pay levels is one where managers feel a particular need for greater flexibility. For middle- and upper-level jobs and those requiring technical expertise, there frequently is a shortage of truly well-qualified personnel. Many managers we interviewed lamented their inability to recruit the best qualified people to these jobs because the rigidities of the compensation plan prevented offering them attractive salaries. This factor also goes hand in hand with the problems of classifying positions "properly," in that usually the classification determines the salary level. It is interesting to note in this context that one of the compensation factors in the questionnaire was "salaries and benefits as compared with those of private industry and other public employers," or comparability. Generally, respondents indicated that the comparability factor had helped the city productivity actions. Follow-up conversations with the city representatives and others convinced us that while these different responses appeared contradictory, in fact they probably were complementary—it appears that respondents, in answering the comparability question, were thinking mostly of comparability of pay and benefits for entry-level and nonmanagerial jobs.

3. *Policies and procedures for rewarding superior performance.* This would appear to us to be one of the most critical of the barriers to productivity improvement. In most of the eight cities, as in many other governments, so-called merit pay increases have become little more than automatic, periodic salary boosts. When supplemented by across-the-board pay adjustments for the rising cost of living, they frequently result in double-digit pay increases annually, with no corresponding increase in performance. There is considerable debate about whether, and to what degree, salary increases and other monetary rewards actually motivate employees to better performance. Nevertheless, there is little doubt that the failure to reward performance (whether by rewarding no one or by rewarding everyone alike) provides a significant disincentive over time.

4. *Policies and procedures for terminating employees "for cause".* This factor, of course, represents one of the customary complaints about government personnel management systems—"They can't even get rid of the total incompetents." Furthermore, it is not clear any longer that this condition is the exclusive domain of the public sector—private firms seem to have considerable

difficulty in terminating nonperforming employees as well. This also could very easily represent an area where much of the problem lies with the managers themselves. Our inquiries showed that operating departments in the eight cities had considerably greater responsibility for terminating employees than the personnel departments or others in the governments.

5. *Procedures for processing promotion, transfer, and termination actions.* It is difficult to explain why respondents felt more negatively about these processing procedures than about some of the other factors in promotions, transfers, and terminations. The reason may be that to many people such processing procedures connote time delays, red tape, and the need to comply with fairly specific rules and regulations.

6. *Number of separate bargaining units.* In theory, this factor could represent too many separate bargaining units or too few. Generally, however, the greatest problems occur because of too many separate units. This factor is not applicable to all the eight cities in the project, since some of them have very little or no bargaining with organized employees. However, in those cities which do engage in collective bargaining, the need to negotiate separately with a number of separate units means additional work, extra costs, and the dangers of "whip-sawing" by the separate bargaining units.

7. *Attitude of unions or employee organizations toward productivity as a bargaining issue.* To some extent, the responses to this factor were predictable because of the survey sample, with its concentration on management personnel in the eight cities. It was beyond the scope of the survey to ask unionized employees the corresponding question about management attitudes, but the responses to such a question could have been interesting. Also, it is not completely clear what kind of union attitude the respondents were reacting to. For example, some of the unions may be very interested in including productivity as a bargaining issue but find that management views productivity as a management prerogative.

The list presented in table 2-5 shows seven additional personnel management factors that appear to have had a generally negative impact on productivity actions in the eight cities, although consensus about the negative effect is not as great as for the seven that were just discussed. These "likely impediments" are personnel management factors that meet the following criteria in terms of respondents' perceptions: (1) the "no impact" responses are less than 50 percent of the total, and (2) the percentage of "impeded" responses is greater than that for "helped."

The Supports

Three personnel management components clearly were perceived by the respondents as supporting their cities' productivity-improvement efforts: performance

Table 2-5
Likely Impediments: Aggregate Percentage Distribution of Responses to Seven Additional Personnel Management Factors

	Impeded	No Impact	Helped
1. "Rule of Three" or other similar selection rules	32.3%	47.0%	20.6%
2. Procedures for establishing or changing fringe benefits	33.6	38.1	28.2
3. Policies on considering seniority in promotions and key lateral transfers	36.1	41.8	22.2
4. Time-in-grade (or similar) requirements for employees to be considered for promotions	34.2	47.6	18.2
5. Labor-management agreement provisions relating to worker productivity	32.2	42.7	25.1
6. Procedures for bargaining process	35.4	40.7	23.9
7. Grievance procedures (collective bargaining)	34.6	37.0	28.4

Note: The distributions reported in this table represent the averages of respondents' ratings of the impact on productivity actions in general of each of the specific factors listed. Individual responses are weighted so that each city's responses count equally.

appraisal, employee development, and employee-employer relations. If one were constructing a list of the personnel management components that theoretically should be the most important for productivity improvement, these three would be on the list. Even so, we were not prepared for the degree of consensus among the respondents about the separate factors within each of the components. At least half the respondents perceived every one of these factors as having helped productivity actions. Table 2-6 displays the percentage distribution of responses on the factors within performance appraisal, employee development, and employee-employer relations.

It is worthwhile to note again, in connection with table 2-6, that respondents' points of reference in answering the questions may have differed considerably. For instance, 64.1 percent indicated that the "procedures for identifying training needs" helped the city productivity actions. Some of the cities may have very precise, well-established needs-identification procedures, which respondents perceived as contributing to the productivity efforts. Other cities may have very general guidelines on how training needs should be identified, which also may have been viewed positively. It is evident, in any case, that respondents were indicating that however they go about identifying training needs, productivity actions were helped by it.

An interesting note about the respondents' perceptions of performance appraisal, employee development, and employee-employer relations is that while they apparently view these components as having a positive effect on

Table 2-6

Supports: Aggregate Percentage Distributions of Responses within Three Personnel Management Components

	Impeded	No Impact	Helped
Performance Appraisal:			
Coverage of the employee performance appraisal system (i.e., proportion of employees included)	13.3%	27.4%	59.3%
Procedures for evaluating employees' performance	22.1	16.4	61.5
Policies or standards for identifying inadequate, acceptable, and superior performance	26.0	14.1	59.8
Established methods of evaluating performance	23.3	14.0	62.6
Average	21.2	18.0	60.8
Employee Development:			
Coverage of formal employee development plan (i.e., proportion of employees included in a plan that identifies the specific training or developmental needs of employees)	19.2	21.2	59.6
Procedures for identifying training needs	18.4	17.6	64.1
Policies and procedures for obtaining training or developmental assignments for employees	20.3	16.1	63.6
Policies or procedures for including training requirements in the planning for productivity-related actions	18.3	23.8	57.9
Encouragements (such as liberal leave policies and tuition payments) for employees to obtain outside training or education	14.5	26.9	58.7
Procedures for matching training to the actual needs of employees	20.6	22.0	57.4
Average	18.6	21.3	60.2
Employee-Employer Relations:			
Established procedures for management consultation with employees in the planning, development, and implementation of productivity actions	23.0	22.5	54.4
Provisions for direct participation by employee representatives in the planning, development, and implementation of productivity actions	22.1	26.1	51.8
Employee attitude toward consulting with management on planning, developing, or implementing productivity actions	33.2	16.7	50.1
Management attitude toward consulting with employees on planning, developing, or implementing productivity actions	34.3	11.0	54.7
Average	28.2	19.1	52.8

Note: The distributions reported in this table represent the averages of respondents' ratings of the impact on productivity actions in general of each of the specific factors listed. Individual responses are weighted so that each city's responses count equally.

productivity improvement, they also seem to feel that too little attention and resources are devoted to them. The following section on potential impacts will provide some documentation of their expressed perceptions through the survey, but we also should mention our own observations. In the oral interviews we had with most of the respondents, several points were made repeatedly, across all cities:

> Most of the respondents felt that their governments generally do a rather poor job of evaluating employees' performance.

> Most respondents acknowledged that they and their governments generally do an inadequate job of ensuring that employees get the training they need to perform their duties at the top of their abilities.

> Many respondents pointed out that in terms of the overall programs, services, and activities of their governments, there actually is relatively little regular consultation with employees.

We mention these general comments in order to make the observation that a little bit of a good thing appears to go a long way.

Two other factors were perceived by a majority of the respondents as having had a positive impact on productivity actions. In the recruitment and selection section, nearly 55 percent of the respondents indicated that the "qualifications of candidates produced by the recruiting efforts" had helped. In compensation, 53.5 percent responded that the "salaries and benefits as compared with those of private industry and other public employers" helped productivity actions. The latter was mentioned earlier—it is our opinion and that of the city representatives to the project that respondents were thinking primarily of pay comparability for entry-level and nonmanagerial jobs in answering this question. On recruitment and selection, it is interesting to see that none of the listed factors was viewed as a clear impediment. The qualifications of candidates is the only output-related factor listed, and it was perceived in a positive light. We should add, however, that this factor was limited to the outputs of recruiting, not including selection of new employees. The fact that an organization apparently recruits good candidates for employment does not mean that it hires the best qualified candidates. Nevertheless, it probably does mean, at least, that it hires good new employees.

Potential Supports

The survey also sought the perceptions of respondents about the potential of the personnel management factors for greater impact on productivity improvement.

Each section of the questionnaire included the following question: Which of the following (classification, compensation, etc.) factors could have provided greater support for the implementation of your city's productivity actions? This question was followed by a request that if the respondent had indicated that more than one factor within the section could have provided greater support, he or she should go back and indicate which one could have provided the greatest support.

1. *Recruitment and selection.* There was strong consensus that two of the factors could have provided greater support, and at least 50 percent felt that each of the other four listed factors could have. On both the "qualifications of candidates produced by the recruiting efforts" and "selection devices/tests and procedures," about 65 percent indicated that there was potential for greater support.

2. *Classification.* Four classification factors were listed in the survey, and all of them were viewed as having the potential for greater support. Consensus was especially strong on two of them. More than 76 percent of the respondents indicated that "procedures for getting positions classified properly" could have provided greater support to the productivity actions. Also, about 67 percent perceived potential support in the "classification standards (the established criteria for use in classifying positions)." However, in selecting the one classification factor that could have provided the greatest support, far more respondents selected the classification procedures.

3. *Compensation.* On one of the compensation factors ("procedures for establishing or changing fringe benefits"), a slight majority of 51.5 percent of the respondents felt that there was no potential for greater support of productivity actions. The other four listed factors were perceived by the majority as capable of greater support. Two of them stand out: 79 percent felt that "policies and procedures for rewarding superior performance (through increased pay or benefits)" could have provided greater support, and 74 percent felt the same about the "relationship of pay levels to the quantity, quality, and degree of difficulty of employees' outputs." Clearly, the most important in the respondents' view was the former—rewards for performance—since a majority picked it as the one factor which could have provided the greatest support.

4. *Performance appraisal.* Four factors were listed, and three of them received substantially positive ratings. The "coverage of the employee performance appraisal system (that is, proportion of employees covered)" was perceived by a majority, however, as lacking the potential for greater support. There was very strong feeling that "policies or standards for identifying inadequate, acceptable, and superior performance" could provide greater support to productivity actions—74 percent answered that it could provide greater support, and over 55 percent chose it for providing the greatest support.

5. *Employee development.* There was very substantial opinion that employee development factors could have provided greater support. Six of the seven factors received 70 percent or greater positive ratings. Correspondingly, there was little consensus on which factors could have provided the greatest

support. The following three factors were the most frequently chosen (with the percentages of respondents by which they were perceived as most important):

Procedures for matching training to the actual needs of employees (29.8 percent)

Coverage of formal employee development plan (that is, proportion of employees included in a plan that identifies the specific training or developmental needs of employees) (17 percent)

Procedures for identifying training needs (17 percent)

6. *Promotions, transfers, and terminations.* There were six factors listed in this section. Respondents thought that three of them could have provided greater support, although on only one of these was the consensus very strong—77 percent responded positively about "policies on considering employee performance in promotions and key lateral transfers." There was very substantial agreement that the other three factors could not have provided greater support for productivity:

Policies on considering seniority in promotions and key lateral transfers (70 percent no)

Time-in-grade (or similar) requirements for employees to be considered for promotions (74 percent no)

"Last-hired, first-fired" (or similar) policies on terminations of employees during reductions in force (75 percent no)

7. *Employee-employer relations.* Five factors were listed in this section, all of them having to do with aspects of involving employee representatives in the planning, development, and implementation of productivity actions. Each of them was perceived by at least 73 percent of the respondents as having the potential for greater impact. Interestingly, there was no apparent consensus among the respondents about which single factor could have provided the greatest support for productivity actions.

8. *Collective bargaining.* As pointed out before, this survey concentrated on management officials and employees. It is not particularly surprising that 80 percent of the respondents felt that the "attitude of unions or employee organizations toward productivity as a bargaining issue" could have provided greater support (62 percent felt that the attitude of management could have helped more). When asked to pick the one factor that could have provided the greatest support, a substantial number (36.5 percent) chose "labor-management agreement provisions relating to worker productivity." The next most frequently selected factor was, again, the attitude of unions (25 percent).

9. *EEO-Affirmative Action.* Generally, the respondents viewed none of the EEO factors as capable of providing greater support. The strongest perception was about "hiring and/or promotion quotas"—72.5 percent of respondents said that quotas could not have provided greater support. EEO is, of course, an emotional issue, and it is not completely clear whether the respondents were answering these questions in terms of specific city programs or experiences or in terms of personal and professional feelings about affirmative action programs generally. In the interviews we had with people in each of the cities, some managers perceived EEO-Affirmative Action purely as a constraint on or complication in their efforts and clearly resented it. Others, however, perceived longer-term payoffs to the government and the citizenry, especially in relation to what we would propose as basic objective number 2 of personnel management: *to assure the responsiveness and responsibility of government workers to the public.* Unlike most of the other personnel management components, EEO-Affirmative Action is not primarily directed at achieving the effectiveness/efficiency objective. (Additional results of the eight-city survey are described in Appendix B.)

Notes

1. Collective bargaining was not an appropriate subject of inquiry in some of the cities, with the absence of any recognized employee unions or organizations. Respondents in those cities were instructed to skip the collective bargaining section.

2. Our definition of personnel staffing levels appears to have been confusing to some of the survey respondents. We have little confidence in the responses to questions about personnel staffing levels and therefore have omitted those results from this book.

3. Standard weighting factors were developed in an effort to have the cities' responses count equally, rather than having the individual respondents' answers count the same. In Tacoma, primarily because of its size and structure of government, 41 persons were surveyed—far more than in any other city. The range for the other seven cities was from 17 to 25 people. A weighting factor was applied to each city's responses. The weighting factors were derived by dividing the smallest number of respondents in a city (17 in Worcester) by each city's total number of respondents. Thus Worcester's weighting factor was 1, or 17 divided by 17, while Tacoma's was 0.4146, or 17 divided by 41. Each response for a city was multiplied by the weighting factor. Appendix B shows all the weighting factors in table B-8.

Appendix 2A
Specific Productivity Actions Referenced in the Eight-City Survey, by City

Dayton, Ohio

1. *Management by Objectives (MBO).* With the MBO system, objectives are established for each program, and completion of these objectives generally occurs as a result of quarterly performance monitoring. As a logical extension of the implementation of MBO, the city manager initiated a performance contract with each department director, and each director is expected to initiate performance contracts with his division heads. The contract states exactly what is expected during the coming year. Future step increases within one's salary range are based on his performance contract.

2. *Reorganization of City Administration.* In January 1976, the city initiated a group management concept. This reorganization saw the creation of three "groups," Administrative Services, Community Services, and Economic Development. This overall reorganization also resulted in the realignment of several departments. By more clearly defining lines of organizational responsibility, the city organization has improved organizational management and accountability.

3. *Project Management.* Project management provides a system which ensures the completion of projects requested by the city commission and/or city manager. It is primarily designed for projects which cross one or more department lines. Projects are assigned to specific departments with a series of specific tasks and deadlines. These deadlines are monitored by the Office of Management and Budget and quarterly reports are prepared for the city manager.

4. *Centralized Accounting.* The city of Dayton moved the accounting function from various operating departments and centralized it in the Department of Finance. This effort has resulted in the reduction of accounting staff throughout the city organization and has allowed the city to take on additional accounting responsibilities without hiring additional staff.

5. *Rerouting Waste Collection.* Recently, the city announced new routes for waste collection. These new routes recognized the changing demographics of the city and were based on the number of pick-ups on each route. As a result, the average daily stops per crew were increased, and the number of crews was decreased from 40 to 35.

6. *Fire Station Location Model.* This year the city of Dayton utilized the Public Technology Institute (PTI) Fire Station Location Model. This model

utilized times and distances between potential fire sources and various potential fire station sites in order to determine the best location for new fire stations.

7. *Geographic Assignment of Housing Inspection.* Housing inspectors are now assigned to individual subneighborhoods within priority board areas. They are supervised at the priority board level. Geographic housing inspection puts housing inspectors closer to the neighborhood, increases the individual inspector's knowledge of the neighborhood, and reduced the number of inspectors from 49 to 34.

Lakewood, Colorado

1. *Program Performance Budgeting System.* This system emphasizes specific program and organizational resource allocation, MBO, program budgeting and evaluation, total resources identification, and allocation.

2. *Municipal Services and Operations Assessment (MSOA).* Policy review and analysis and organizational and manpower assessment.

3. *Organizational Development.* Team building within and between all levels of management.

4. *Employee Planning and Review System.* Establishing objectives and review performance of each city employee semiannually and annually.

5. *Council Committee System (and Pending Council Items).* Coordination of issues brought to attention of Council—transportation, safety, development, and finance and operations.

Nashville-Davidson, Tennessee

1. *The Productivity Awards Program.* The productivity improvement committee developed a metrowide awards program to reward employees submitting suggestions on how to improve productivity. Suggestions for improvement are turned in, evaluated, and selected for implementation. Bonds were given to the award recipients on suggestions such as recycled computer paper, water heater timers, etc.

2. *Metro Postal and Messenger Service.* A metro postal and messenger service has been established to pick up and deliver mail and messages from one centralized location. Mail, both internal and external, is picked up and delivered twice each work day from strategically located boxes and offices. Most metro agencies and departments participate in the service, increasing both effectiveness and efficiency.

3. *Budgeting of Computer Services.* Data processing and services now operates as a profit center. Charges are made directly to user departments according to the amount of services provided. These charges are estimated and

included in individual departmental and agency budgets, which causes a closer evaluation of actual services required.

4. *Police Effectiveness and Efficiency Assessment.* Because of increasing rates of crime, the police department has implemented programs to increase police effectiveness and assess efficiency of its personnel. Programs address the behavior of police officers, quality of report writing, improved court demeanor skills, and improved quality of arrests. Preventive walking patrols downtown and in community target areas have been established, using hand-held radios.

5. *Emergency Ambulance Service Center.* Fire Engine Company No. 6 was moved to equip another new station and the vacated building converted to a centralized emergency ambulance service center. This allowed all services, communications, training, supplies, and other related functions to be pulled together at one location. This center has enabled metro to develop a very effective emergency ambulance and rescue service, providing for the total community.

6. *Land Information System.* An innovative computerized land information system is being developed to provide common land parcel information to multiple metro departments and agencies. The information is available to the users as needed. Some 30 terminals are located across metro to access the land bank system, which will include tax assessment data, ownership, cost, buildings, streets, utilities, and other basic related data.

St. Paul, Minnesota

1. *Change in City Charter.* The change was from the commission form to the strong mayor form. Productivity was to improve by virtue of centralizing administrative authority in the mayor, who is responsible for the efficiency of city operations. One of the resulting changes is a more open and understandable budget process.

2. *Unified Capital Improvement Budget Process.* The new decision-making process will be fully implemented in 1977. The objective is to have one process which selects capital projects regardless of fund source. The process will require more information and better coordination on projects. The new process also requires more citizen involvement in the proposing and selecting of projects.

3. *Training Program, Including Performance Appraisal.* The new program is being implemented by the training coordinator. The first phase is supervisory training so that the new performance appraisal system may be utilized. The objective is to increase productivity through better communications, and formal appraisal, between workers and supervisors.

4. *Licensing Division Consolidation.* The objective of this change was to eliminate duplication and unnecessary functions. The result is the centralization of most licenses in one office, the creation of standard procedures, and the drafting of a uniform license ordinance.

5. *Elimination of the Office of Emergency Preparedness.* A cost-effectiveness study was performed on the functions of the office to determine whether the functions were necessary, and whether city expenditures were justified. The result was to name the fire chief the director of emergency preparedness, with some additional responsibilities, and to transfer the remaining employees to other positions.

6. *Elimination of the Office of Consumer Affairs.* A study was performed to determine whether the functions of the office could be performed by the State Division of Consumer Protection. The result was to transfer one employee to the state division, one to another city office, while another voluntarily left city employment. The office was closed and the state now handles city complaints.

Savannah, Georgia

1. *Responsive Public Services Program (RPSP).* The city of Savannah initiated the Responsive Public Services Program in the spring of 1974 as an effort to determine the effectiveness of public services in meeting community needs. The findings of the RPSP were published in August 1974 and were based on survey and research work which (1) updated previously collected data, (2) served as a source of information on additional service activities, and (3) developed further the methodology for measuring service effectiveness. While no extensive surveys have been conducted since the report, the data base is updated periodically through departmental reports. The RPSP represents a citywide effort to monitor eleven community conditions: cleanliness, crime prevention, dog control, fire prevention, flood hazard, housing, land use, recreation use, street conditions, street signs, and water and sewer adequacy.

2. *Fleet Management Improvements.* As a result of the work of a study team appointed in 1974 to look into the problem of sharply rising maintenance cost of city vehicles, 1975 costs showed a savings over 1974. Continuing studies and identification of problem vehicles and operations resulted in 1976 costs being held to the 1975 level and below 1974 with much improved vehicle availability for certain fleets. System changes will be extended to other fleets in 1977.

3. *Modular Classification and Pay System.* The city and a consulting firm have developed a modular classification and pay system for several operational areas. The module provides a means for an individual to enter an occupational grouping and increase in job skills, performance, and achievement and receive corresponding rewards. Police and fire were selected as the first areas of implementation. Substantial training materials have been developed and distributed to the employees in these departments.

4. *Resource Management System.* The city of Savannah decided to launch a series of studies as part of an ongoing attempt to construct an integrated management control system linking budgeting, scheduling, reporting, and

productivity improvements. This program commenced in 1977. Inhouse analytical staff are being trained in industrial engineering/resource management techniques by outside consultants. It is anticipated there will be annualized savings of between 2 and 15 percent for the entire general fund.

Scottsdale, Arizona

1. *Mechanized Refuse Collection.* The city of Scottsdale has pioneered mechanized refuse collection. Mechanized collection means that refuse is deposited in large polyethylene containers by the customers, a refuse truck then picks up the container and dumps the contents into the truck body mechanically.

2. *Contracted Fire Services.* Fire protection in Scottsdale is a combined public- and private-sector effort under private management. The city owns over half the equipment and all of Scottsdale's four fire stations. The city furnishes cross-trained city employees to supplement the department's full-time fire fighters. Rural-metro provides full-time administrative personnel, maintenance, full-time fire fighters, and the remainder of the suppression equipment.

3. *Program Evaluation.* The city of Scottsdale has developed a process for selecting city operating programs—such as refuse collection and parks maintenance—and then identifying the program's objectives and measuring the success in accomplishing the objectives. Program evaluation requires program managers to state their objectives and holds them accountable for results.

4. *Objective Setting, Measurement, and Program Review.* Each year the city council adopts general city priorities. Then, the city departments prepare operating objectives within the guidelines of the adopted priorities. Objectives are measured and reported in program review meetings with the city manager. The objectives become the basis for preparing annual budget estimates.

5. *Team Management.* The city has developed the concept of team management because many problems may be caused by fragmentation and lack of communication. The goal of team management is to establish priorities of administration and/or policy according to the overall needs of the city of Scottsdale. A management team may include any combination of members either from a single department or from several departments, depending on the type of problem to be solved or project to be completed.

6. *Team Policing.* The concept of team policing is based on the "officer on the beat." Three teams have permanently assigned officers who have personally assigned responsibility for a designated geographic area.

Tacoma, Washington

1. *Performance/Program Budgeting, Management by Objectives.* The city of Tacoma is in the process of developing a program budgeting system.

Management by objectives is incorporated into the process. For the past 3 years, Tacoma has operated under a dual budgeting system. Two annual budgets are prepared: the administrative or line-item budget and the program budget. The preliminary budget is reviewed and balanced by the budget review team, which is composed of six department directors representing the major areas of the city government. The program budget will provide the city of Tacoma government with a tool for program planning and evaluation.

2. *Organizational Development.* The objectives and purposes of the organizational development program are to improve communication among the top administrators and to induce them to think through city problems and find solutions through working together. This process has produced the management team, which is composed of the department directors and its subcommittee the budget review team. The management team acts as an advisory body to the city manager. Many problems are resolved with temporary teams composed of top administrators and staff from several departments. The vanishing concept is used—once a problem is resolved, the team is dismantled. On the other hand, many other teams are permanent, with rotating membership.

3. *Productivity Bargaining.* Both the city of Tacoma government and city employee unions are prominently involved in supporting productivity clauses in labor-management agreements. The purpose of the productivity clauses is to directly involve employees in finding more productive ways of working. Turning back part of the savings to employees provides strong incentive to use resources with maximum effectiveness. The city currently has negotiated productivity clauses with its fire fighters and refuse department crews.

4. *Five-Inch Hose, Quick-Release Couplings.* The adoption of 5-inch hose and quick-release couplings by the fire department is a technological-innovation (hardware) project of the city government. The fire department has used the new technology and a *siting model* analysis to reduce eleven fire fighters from attack companies and to make utilization of the remaining manpower.

5. *Automatic Hydrant Valve.* This is another technological-innovation (hardware) project of the city government. The valve will allow a fire fighter to open a hydrant from the nozzle instead of at the hydrant. This will allow one more "man on the job" to fight the fire.

6. *Geo-based Coding System.* Another technological-innovation (hardware) project, this system will provide a computerized "city map" indicating locations of utility service lines, buildings, streets, and other basic information necessary to the operating of city departments. The system will also provide a valuable tool for city government planning and decision making.

Worcester, Massachusetts

1. *Capital Improvement Project.* A project undertaken by the budget officer and the city's Office of Planning and Community Development,

establishing, on a formal and recurring basis, a 5-year capital program integrated with the annual budget cycle. The capital plan also specifies in detail the proposed financing and an analysis of the debt structure.

2. *Centralization of Data Processing.* The city established a staff department in order to centralize all data-processing activities into one agency, said agency to serve as a service bureau for all municipal departments. Eventually, other agencies' data-processing activities will be ended.

3. *Police Service Aide Project.* Forty-five civilian aides were hired for the police department to perform non-law-enforcement duties handled by police officers so as to permit police officers to concentrate on law enforcement tasks. In addition, specialized police squads were created for robbery and burglary, and a crime prevention unit was formed to support these activities.

4. *Sanitation Division Improvement Project.* The operations of the sanitation division were analyzed and new work practices and procedures were established in order to carry on the same level of sanitation service with less personnel, as a result of budget cuts. Improvements included the study of routes and the change in tasks performed by sanitation men.

5. *Consolidation of Code Inspection.* A new code inspection department was established in order to consolidate inspectional activities within one agency so as to permit better coordination and allocation of inspection resources.

6. *Public Works Patching Project.* A new type of patching material has been developed in order to attempt to create a cold patch which will have sustained holding power in connection with filling of potholes in streets during winter months.

3

Performance of Personnel Management

There have been very few efforts to assess or evaluate the overall productivity or performance of personnel management in municipal governments. Some cities have attempted to evaluate the performance of their personnel departments or offices, but those studies generally have been confined to just a few personnel functions, such as recruitment or classification. Moreover, they have taken little, if any, note of the critical relationships between the personnel office and the many other aspects of, and actors in, personnel management in the government. It is easy to fall into the trap of thinking that what goes on in a personnel office is the entirety of personnel management.

PSL asked the representatives of the eight cities participating in the project to complete a short inquiry about various personnel management functions and who is responsible for them in their governments. They were encouraged to consult as appropriate with the personnel directors, civil service commissions, department heads, city managers, and others in order to answer the questions accurately. The responses show that line departments overall have about the same degree of responsibility for the personnel management functions as the central personnel offices. There was, of course, some variation between cities. The responses, averaged for the whole group of cities, are shown in table 3-1.

Productivity improvement in personnel management services requires a definition initially of the responsibilities for such management. To illustrate the danger of looking only at a personnel office, one may consider how new employees frequently are hired in local governments. First, a new position is requested and then authorized, which might involve the line manager, budget officer, personnel director, city manager or chief executive, and, in some cases, the elected council. Next, a position description, appropriate classification, salary level, and qualification requirements are determined, again perhaps involving the line manager, personnel director, and city manager (and usually others as well). Finally, a recruiting request is initiated, candidates are examined, rated, and certified, final candidates are interviewed, a selection is made, and the new employee is appointed (probably by the city manager, upon the recommendation of the manager of an agency). In the course of hiring one new employee, as many as ten or more city officials and workers probably have been involved.

Personnel management in a city government comprises much more than the operations of the personnel office and/or civil service commission. It is, as we see it, a set of discrete but closely related programs, practices, policies,

37

Table 3-1

Degrees of Responsibility for Various Components of Personnel Management
(*average of ratings from eight cities*)

	Central Personnel Office	Civil Service Commission	Operating Departments	City Manager/ Mayor
Recruitment and selection	1.4	0.6	0.8	0.6
Classification	2.3	0.3	0.4	0.4
Compensation	2.4	0.1	0.3	0.5
Performance appraisal	1.3	0.3	1.8	0.5
Employee development	1.3	0.1	1.6	0.6
Promotions	0.5	–	2.0	0.9
Transfers	0.7	–	1.8	0.9
Terminations	0.7	0.1	1.8	0.9
Collective bargaining	0.8	0.1	0.5	1.0
EEO-Affirmative Action	1.1	0.1	0.8	1.0
Overall average	1.3	0.1	1.2	0.7

Key to ratings: Scale 0 = No responsibility
1 = Somewhat responsible
2 = Principally responsible
3 = Solely responsible

and decisions, all concerned with the government's human resources. Personnel management depends on numerous employees and officials throughout the government organization.

Many governments in recent years have undertaken to assess the effectiveness of various programs. They also have sought to evaluate the performance of their employees, but without linking the two assessments. Cities that have developed measures of program outputs have a basis for relating those program outputs to the work of staff. Three general cases of outputs may be distinguished—for both programs and workers. The first case comprises those programs and workers whose jobs involve direct contact with the citizens, as in the case of teachers in schools or doctors in clinics. The second case involves the provision or achievement of definable, measurable services or products, such as smooth road and highway surfaces or safe drinking water. The third case includes all the programs and workers who neither have direct contact with citizen-clients nor deliver an easily definable service or product. In the first two cases, performance can be assessed in terms of the satisfaction of the clients or against some objective, observable standard. The third case, however, requires a wholly different kind of assessment, one that relates to the *impact* that those programs and workers have *on the government's ability to achieve its missions*. The common technique of measuring workloads or processes of the third-case workers and programs is not sufficient for any realistic assessment of their performance.

Personnel management is included in the third-case programs, in that personnel management programs and policies do not provide direct services or products to the citizenry but rather are involved in ensuring that the government has the capability to provide services and products efficiently and effectively.

A first step toward assessing the performance of personnel management and other third-case programs is to identify their objectives. If what is supposed to be accomplished is not defined, no one can determine whether it is being accomplished.

The Basic Personnel Management Objectives

Almost everyone has heard it said that the aim of modern public personnel management is to ensure merit in all aspects of employment. This, however, is a confusion of means with ends. The aim of personnel management in government is not simply to maintain merit employment practices. The National Civil Service League, which was instrumental in writing and passing the 1883 Pendleton Act that established the Federal Civil Service (the model for many states and localities), has noted:

> Many of the methods by which governments have contrived to assure merit employment and protect the service against past abuses have also served to exclude many well-qualified persons, severely limit the flexibility of responsible elected officials, and curtail the overall effectiveness of public service.[1]

And more recently, the National Academy of Public Administration (in a review of the Intergovernmental Personnel Act grant program) has observed:

> Effective public services must be the ultimate test of effective public servants. To put it another way, the ultimate test of an effective personnel system must be effective personnel or effective public management. If a personnel system satisfies all the ideal standards of the personnel profession in selecting, classifying, and rewarding personnel who yet fail to deliver effective public services, it is a hollow shell, a form without substance. The purpose of improving personnel systems is to improve public services by improving public management.[2]

Working with the city representatives to this project and the Advisory Panel, we have identified three basic purposes or objectives of personnel management in a government: (1) to provide the human resources required for effective and efficient delivery of needed services to the public, (2) to assure the responsiveness and responsibility of government workers to the citizenry, and

(3) to provide leadership in maintaining and improving the quality of working life. They are presented essentially in order of priority; that is, the most important aim of personnel management is to ensure that the government has the workforce capability to provide services to the public effectively and efficiently.

Personnel management can be seen also as the composite of various interrelated subsystems or components, each of which has its own, more limited objectives. In a rationally organized system of personnel management, the combined effect of these components should be the achievement of the basic personnel management objectives.

In the course of this project, PSL published a guidebook for city officials called *Assessing Personnel Management: Objectives and Performance Indicators.*[3] Joining as co-sponsors of the publication were the U.S. Conference of Mayors, National League of Cities, and International Personnel Management Association. The idea behind the guidebook is to suggest to top city officials a useful framework for reviewing personnel management performance in their governments. The guide contains the preceding listing of basic personnel management objectives and discusses possible indicators of progress toward achieving them. It also identifies potential objectives of each of the components of personnel management and illustrative indicators of performance for those subobjectives.

Some of those illustrative materials are reproduced in appendix 3A at the end of this chapter. Many of the indicators are presented as "open" criteria for assessment. They are intended only to illustrate types of existing or easily obtainable information that could be used in assessing progress toward the component objectives, not how that information should be interpreted. There is no way to develop a standard set of indicators with precise instructions on how to interpret them that would be appropriate for use in all city governments. The diversity among cities and their leadership is much too great. The organizational goals of the government must be the focal point of all management actions, and each city must determine those goals for itself. Foulkes and Morgan have presented this same observation in relation to evaluating personnel management in corporations:

> The best personnel policies for Polaroid, Xerox, or IBM arise from different contexts from those for U.S. Steel, Kennecott Copper, and the Ford Motor Company. Good personnel policies must be judged by how well they serve the particular management and employees. Do they work? Are they easy to understand and implement? Do they contribute to the attainment of corporate goals? . . .
>
> Good personnel policies cannot stand apart from the basic strategies of the organization as a whole.[4]

Determining Effectiveness

Much work needs to be done to assess the productivity of personnel management. In theory, the most accurate way to measure personnel management effectiveness in a city government would be to examine the contribution of personnel management practices and policies to each of the separate programs and services of the government. Our earlier statements of the basic personnel management objectives are based on the general organizational goals of a government: effective and efficient delivery of needed services, responsiveness and responsibility to the citizens, and leadership in the quality of working life. In addition, the individual programs and service-delivery mechanisms of a government have their own operating objectives that should be reflective of the overall government goals. A comprehensive review of personnel management effectiveness would require the assessment of personnel management's impact on the objectives of each of these individual programs.

For example, in a paper prepared for the National Association of Tax Administrators,[5] we noted that the effectiveness of personnel management policies and practices should be reviewed in terms of the city or state tax agency's specific aims. These aims might include:

1. To provide a high quality of service to the public, including:

   a. Courteous response, with due regard for the dignity of each inquirer and without regard to color, social status, or any other personal factors
   b. Prompt response to all inquiries
   c. Knowledgeable and accurate responses
   d. Certainty about tax liability
   e. Honesty
   f. Concern for the cost of tax compliance

2. To achieve efficient and equitable collection of all appropriate tax monies (including tax appeal mechanisms, absence of corruption, information services to taxpayers)
3. To provide competent advice to legislators and executive policymakers on revenue expectations and potential new sources of revenue
4. To provide a work environment that is conducive to the safety, personal and career development, and satisfaction of individual employees

How well do the government's personnel management policies, programs, and practices contribute to the achievement of these tax administration objectives? How well do they contribute to the achievement of the objectives of each of the government's other programs or services? Such a series of evaluative reviews would be required to reach a comprehensive appraisal of personnel management effectiveness in a particular city government. However, this does not mean that such a procedure is required in practice to determine personnel management performance. On the contrary, such an effort would almost surely be doomed, because it would be overly complicated and time consuming.

Less comprehensive examinations are more practical and can produce meaningful and usable results. There are three basic techniques or processes that are appropriate for looking at performance or productivity. While there are significant differences between them, the three techniques are fundamentally similar, in that all of them are question-posing, answer-seeking processes.

The first, which may be called *assessment*, is concerned mainly with the general effectiveness of the programs and policies under review. An assessment of personnel management may be defined as a broad-scaled management review, aimed at beginning to determine the general effectiveness and adequacy of personnel management programs and policies in relation to the human-resource needs of the organization.

Evaluation is concerned with determining whether what was planned or expected to happen has in fact occurred. A useful definition is that evaluation "attempts to appraise and measure the actual inputs, processes, outcomes, and operational settings of . . . ongoing programs or policies in order to compare these findings with those which were anticipated or assumed."[6]

Finally, *analysis* is a more problem-oriented technique, concerned with both effects and costs of policies and programs. Analysis "searches for alternative policies and programs for achieving public objectives and attempts to assess and compare their anticipated costs and benefits over time, as well as their other consequences, in order to provide the basis for better future choices."[7]

In the following sections of this chapter, we discuss significant aspects of each of the three techniques in relation to public personnel management. Complementary to these sections is the material developed and described in chapter 4 on the costs of personnel management.

Personnel Management Assessment

An initial assessment should not require expensive data collection and manipulation. Rather, the intention is to use existing information, already available or easily obtainable, to expand knowledge in four basic areas of concern:

1. Are the personnel management policies and programs creating problems in meeting the staffing requirements of the government? The government should try to determine whether the basic personnel management objectives are being met and whether there are any important shortcomings.

2. Do the personnel management policies and practices reflect the values of the elected leaders and the community of citizens? The issues in personnel management today involve basic policy questions that go beyond job classification, recruitment policies, and salary schedules. The objectives of personnel management must reflect the values of the community and particularly those of the elected leadership. A series of political and social issues confront elected officials in the staffing of the government. Examples of such issues include:

What are the rights of employees to job tenure, and why?

Should employees participate in political party activities?

What are the attitudes toward employee unions?

Should employees have to meet residency requirements?

What are the government's responsibilities in the employment of minorities and other special groups—the blind, the handicapped, veterans, and women?

Should pay increases be automatic?

Should government workers be paid more, less, or about the same as comparable workers in the private sector?

These and other basic issues cannot be decided simply by reference to a personnel rule or regulation. Staffing policies must necessarily be harmonized with the community's values.

3. Are the vital personnel management roles being filled properly?

a. *Elected officials and senior administrators.* Do top officials, in making policy and program decisions, analyze the staffing implications or the impact on employee morale and performance?

b. *Managers and supervisors.* Do program managers and supervisors understand and fulfill their responsibilities for personnel management? Do they treat personnel problems as the government's problems (that is, sharing the responsibility), or do they treat them as the problems of the personnel staff ("I'm a program manager, personnel is *their* problem")?

c. *The personnel director and staff.* Are the personnel director and staff clearly a part of the city's overall management team? Are they part of the main policy and program decision-making structure? Do they contribute to the early stages of the city's program planning?

d. *City employees.* Do city employees understand the nature of the services they and their agencies are providing? Do they understand their role in providing those services? Do they understand that in many cases they are the representatives of the city to the public and that the whole city government may be judged by their actions? Are city workers listened to in the formulation of policies that affect them directly? Are employees encouraged to make suggestions to improve the system?

4. Are the major personnel management subobjectives being achieved? An illustrative listing of major personnel management subobjectives is presented in appendix 3A at the end of this chapter. It is important that the government spell out as clearly as possible the major purposes of the personnel management programs and policies and determine, at least roughly, whether they are being met. Further analysis and evaluation of subsystems of personnel management will be required to gain the information needed about alternative methods for achieving the subobjectives.

The careful identification of objectives and selection of performance indicators is the key step in an assessment (just as it is for evaluation and analysis). Each jurisdiction necessarily will define the overall aims of personnel management in its own terms. The listing of three major personnel management objectives presented earlier might be representative.

Beyond the assessment of progress toward the basic objectives of personnel management, review of the component subobjectives is also necessary. Objectives and criteria are required for each of the relatively discrete, although closely related, components of personnel management (for example, recruitment and selection, compensation, employee development). Breaking down personnel management into its principal components will make the identification of subobjectives easier. (Appendix 3A, at the end of this chapter, illustrates a possible breakdown of the components.)

Usable indicators are needed to assess performance and determine whether the stated objectives and subobjectives are being achieved. The indicators should define the information needed to determine the direction and rate of progress in meeting the objectives. It is important to remember that an assessment is mainly concerned with the effectiveness of the personnel system or its components (whether the objectives are being met). In selecting performance indicators, the following criteria are important:

Do the indicators encompass the entire objective as stated?

Are the indicators subject to measurement by recent and reliable (and preferably recurrent) information?

Is the information required by the indicators already available? If not, are the costs of data collection reasonable in terms of the size and significance of the objective?

Will the indicators (and the information that supports them) be clear to potential users?

The indicators provided in appendix 3A generally draw on information that is usually available or easily obtainable in most governments. Initial indicators must be functional, even though they may fall somewhat short of measuring the total performance. Over time, government officials are likely to seek greater clarity and specificity, and the cost of new measurements will have to be evaluated against the usefulness of their applications.

Information on the indicators provides a basis for assessing the progress toward the appropriate objectives. Is the objective being met? If not, are the relevant programs and policies coming close to meeting the objective?

An assessment of personnel management performance can produce several benefits. For one thing, officials gain a clearer perception of how the pieces or components of personnel management fit together and, in many cases, are interdependent. For another, the documentation is provided to achieve a broader understanding of the roles of various officials in accomplishing personnel management objectives. In addition, the government should gain a fairly good perception of whether the personnel management programs and policies are performing as needed. Where the performance is inadequate, the information compiled provides at least a rough idea of where the trouble spots are and of the more specific personnel management issues that require analysis.

A successful assessment of personnel management performance depends, to a large extent, on the following organizational conditions:

Ensure top-level support. For an assessment to start on firm footing and have any importance, the top policymakers and administrators must be committed to it and give it support. This top-level involvement should include elected officials.

Involve as many people as possible or practical. It is extremely important that senior administrators and their staffs cooperate in the effort. Any review or assessment is likely to be threatening to some people, but their concerns may be allayed by an open, participatory review of policies and programs.

Designate a core staff. An inhouse core staff that can devote a major portion of its time and attention to the assessment is necessary. The staff can provide a focal point for the effort and help ensure that needed information is compiled, that the schedule is met, and that everyone is kept involved and informed.

Evaluation

In recent years, all levels of government have been under continuous and increasing pressure to evaluate public policies and programs to demonstrate their effectiveness. This pressure is a public demand for accountability, and in most instances it has had a positive influence on the conduct of government. However, human resource and personnel management policies and programs are considerably behind other segments of government in evaluation. The move to encourage evaluation and greater accountability centered first on functional program areas, leaving administrative services and internal management policies and programs as a later concern.

An intensive examination by the Public Services Laboratory of research dealing with personnel management in city governments included a search for evaluations of pay methods, promotion, firing and transfer practices, recruitment and selection, classification, retirement systems, productivity incentives, affirmative action, and collective bargaining.[8] This search showed that little existed by way of hard evaluation of city staffing policies and programs. Even in the case of employee training, few studies followed through from the act of training to changes in performance on the job. Economic wage-impact analysis of collective bargaining showed little in the way of wage differentials from union bargaining between government and the industrial sector, yet underscored the weaknesses of existing research. Public-sector job evaluations pointed mostly to the need for greater clarification of purpose and more study.

Nevertheless, with the experience of setting the framework for evaluation already behind most governments, there is now the capacity to turn attention to such concerns as personnel management policies and programs. Indeed, both external and internal pressures may make it necessary.

A number of ways are available to improve the climate for evaluation of personnel management policies and programs, such as:

1. Specifically including evaluation as part of any study of, or recommendation for, change in personnel management methods. Thus, if a new incentive award is introduced, evaluation machinery might be incorporated from the outset (together with the clarity and specification of objectives and criteria for measurement that are essential to evaluation).

2. Setting aside resources of staff and funds to permit evaluation studies to be carried out. The location of such an evaluation unit and its specialization depend on the number of city employees and the complexity of the human resource problems. Unless the resources are at a reasonable level, however, the work will not go forward even if a formal evaluation requirement is imposed.

3. Implementing processes that explicitly provide for the consideration of evaluation studies and their subsequent findings by employees, unions, and the public. Unless the employees who have an interest in evaluation studies participate in their formulation, conduct, and analysis, and in the subsequent actions to amend ongoing practices, the necessary cooperation for implementation will be difficult to secure. Timing of efforts to gain participation both of employees and (for the major issues) the public necessarily remains an administrative art, not unlike other administrative timing problems. In general, however, early discussions with personnel and unions is essential to subsequent acceptance of actual evaluation findings.

4. Routinely incorporating staffing concerns related to program policies in all program evaluation efforts, particularly in project monitoring. Personnel resources—the number and quality of employees, including their abilities and motivation—are a major determinant of the government's output, the services to people. If programs "worked," in terms of efficient and effective service delivery, what input of staff resources made them work? If they did not, what, if any, input of staff resources was at fault? Did the employees understand the purpose and nature of the services they and their program were providing? Did the several groups of employees understand their particular roles? Did the

employees have a chance to comment on or make suggestions? Did personnel regulations interfere with the success of the program policy? Once the staffing problems are diagnosed, it would be desirable to suggest alternative staffing measures among the corrective options to be considered in subsequent analyses.

Analysis of Personnel Management Issues

As defined earlier, analysis is a questioning process that seeks to determine what alternative means of accomplishing an objective exist and to compare the probable costs and benefits of the various options. In dealing with public personnel management and the staffing issues of government, analysis is two dimensional. First, there is a personnel policy dimension, which is concerned with specific personnel policies, procedures, or programs and their alternatives. Second, there is the government program dimension, in which the primary concern is a particular functional program, but the analysis must deal with the personnel aspects of the various program options.

In one form or another, much analysis of programs and policies is going on in state and local governments, and analytic processes are frequently built into new program formulation. However, the personnel impacts in program formulation are often neglected. Analysis of these personnel-related aspects of priority policy issues can help avoid many of the irritants that weaken employees' motivation and pride in their work. For instance, budget decisions may mandate cutbacks in staff levels, but the decisions about such cutbacks might neglect consideration of ways to ease the transition, such as job referrals or retraining. Terminations that are crudely and inconsiderately carried out can destroy morale and raise the unit costs of government service instead of reducing costs as intended.

The initial step in analysis is the careful identification of the issue or problem. The intent is simply to state the questions being raised straightforwardly, making clear the starting point of the cost-effectiveness analysis and putting the study in context. The broad-scaled assessment of personnel management which was previously discussed is a useful method of highlighting personnel management issues and problem areas that warrant detailed analysis. Once the issue has been agreed upon, there follows a series of closely connected and related steps toward completion of a cost-effectiveness analysis. These steps are summarized below.

Summary statement defining the problem. The formulation of the real problem is a difficult and critical step. To help get at that problem, considerable information may need to be assembled. The information may be displayed in a summary way, starting with a statement of the questions as they appear to be raised in the initial round of consideration and followed by a description of the essential features of the problem. The aim is to define the problem and its size, and to expose the issues and topics which seem most in need of analysis. Because so many choices have to be made in the course of an analysis—both at this stage and later on—and because these choices can have such a high content of value judgment, there must be (1) explicit statement of the reasons for choices, (2) review by interested agencies in the early stages, and (3) participation by the ultimate policy officials as early and as often as possible.

Identification of basic objectives. The formulation of program or policy objectives is aided greatly by the identification of the nature and scope of the problem. Can the problem be prevented (for example, employee resignations)? What would be the purpose of preventive methods (for example, lower turnover costs, including costs of recruitment and hiring, training, etc.)? It has been so customary to define program and policy objectives, particularly in personnel management, in terms of means of administration or of meeting staffing requirements that special emphasis should be given to defining objectives as ends desired by the people served by the government or the clients of the government personnel.

Further, it is important that the objectives be framed to include all the implications that need to be considered in choosing the major alternative means of accomplishing the objectives. Not all the relevant factors may be capable of measurement, but it is essential initially that even the unquantifiable judgmental factors be identified so that they can be taken into account. Specifically,

An objective statement should capture the full impact that is intended (including "quality" aspects that may be hard to measure).

An objective should be limited to the impact that is possible.

An objective statement should take note of potential adverse impacts (for example, "to accomplish x without causing y to happen").

Selection of criteria, or measures of effectiveness. The aim is to devise common yardsticks that can be applied to the alternative approaches, to see what can be expected of each of them toward the achievement of stated objectives. As far as possible, criteria should be selected that are capable of quantitative measurement. Criteria for measuring program or policy effectiveness should be selected for how much they tell about program operation and should be related as closely as possible to the basic objectives. (See also the discussion of indicators in the earlier section on assessments.)

Identification of major alternatives or options. The generation of options is crucial to any analytic effort. Essentially, the generation of options helps to avoid "locking-in" a single, traditional approach to meeting a problem and to stimulate an imaginative search for innovative ways of satisfying the identified needs and purposes.

Optional methods might be found by drawing on the experience of other governments through the compilations of associations of governments and other public interest organizations or the various information systems about city and state programs administered by federal government agencies. The employees of a government also may generate options that fit the particular problem. In fact, participation by operating-level officials and employees is essential, not only because of their familiarity with the operational details, but also because their participation is necessary to the effective implementation of any decision that is reached.

An example may serve to underscore the option-generation process. An objective may be to increase police surveillance in one or more areas of the city. Several types of options might include:

To reduce staffing of individual cruising vehicles to one officer per vehicle

To take police officers off desk duty and assign them to surveillance tasks

To recruit and train additional police officers

To develop a neighborhood volunteer corps for observation and periodic reporting to neighborhood patrol officers

To increase use of television and other communication equipment

Most, if not all, of these options would require some change in the way the workforce is used and in the training requirements.

Analysis is not meaningful without defined program or policy options. The backbone of analysis is the comparison of options that have been generated—comparison of information on both the costs of alternatives and their relative effectiveness in satisfying the defined objectives.

Estimation of the costs and effectiveness of the alternatives. Cost estimates must be made for each program or policy alternative considered in order to determine how much of the jurisdiction's limited resources each would require, both initially and over some projected future period of operation. Estimates of the returns that may reasonably be expected from each program alternative can then be weighed against the resource allocation required. In order to estimate the costs of alternatives, it is necessary to have fairly detailed information about the operational aspects and activities involved in the proposal. (More about personnel management costs is presented in chapter 4.)

Estimation of effectiveness lies at the heart of analysis—pulling together all the information possible about the probable accomplishments of each alternative. Fairly reliable knowledge about the results that can be expected from each of the possible approaches increases the likelihood that the course of action chosen will have the most impact for the level of resources that the jurisdiction is able and willing to devote to that particular purpose.

Estimates will have to be linked to the program criteria selected earlier, and as the work of data collection goes forward, it may well be that some revision of the selected criteria will become desirable. However, even rough estimates will increase the opportunity for more informed choices.

Notes

1. National Civil Service League, *Model Public Personnel Administration Law* (Washington, D.C.: National Civil Service League, November 1970).

2. Panel of the National Academy of Public Administration, *Improving Personnel Management in State and Local Government: A Review of the Grants Program of the Intergovernmental Personnel Act* (Washington, D.C.: March 1976), p. 57.

3. Selma J. Mushkin and Frank H. Sandifer, *Assessing Personnel Management: Objectives and Performance Indicators* (Washington, D.C.: Public Services Laboratory, Georgetown University, March 1977).

4. Fred K. Foulkes and Henry M. Morgan, "Organizing and Staffing the Personnel Function," *Harvard Business Review* 55(3):146, May-June 1977. Copyright © 1977 by the President and Fellows of Harvard College; all rights reserved.

5. Selma J. Mushkin and Frank H. Sandifer, "Productivity in Tax Administration: Personnel Management Factors," in *Public Personnel Administration—Policies and Practices for Personnel*, Report Bulletin 6, Vol. 5 (Englewood Cliffs, N.J.: Prentice Hall, 1977), pp. 531-533.

6. U.S. General Accounting Office, *Evaluation and Analysis to Support Decision-Making*, PAD-76-9 (Washington, D.C.: U.S. Government Printing Office, 1976).

7. Ibid.

8. Public Services Laboratory, *Staffing Services to People in the Cities: A Series of Research Reviews*, Nos. 1-10 (Washington, D.C.: Public Services Laboratory, Georgetown University, 1975).

Appendix 3A
Illustrative Subobjectives of Personnel Management and Indicators of Progress Toward Their Achievement

I. Classification and Staffing Levels

A. Subobjective: To maintain an accurate and up-to-date inventory of the kinds and levels of jobs in the government and establish appropriate staffing levels.

Indicators

1. Are there forecasts of staffing levels by occupation and classification?
2. Number and proportion of positions covered in the classification plan.
3. Percentage of job classes capable of being described in terms of the kinds of outputs produced by the employees, and percentage actually described in that way (e.g., numbers of people served, number of treatments provided, tons of trash collected, etc.).
4. Percentage of jobs and job classes which have been subject to complete job analysis within the past 3 years.
5. Number and percentage of agency requests for reclassifications met within a specified time.

B. Subobjective: To outline career progressions (ladders) in order to encourage employees to strive for high performance.

Indicators

1. Number and percentage of employees (at specified classes) who are upgraded on the basis of job performance.
2. Percentage of employees within sample job classes who progressed to higher level jobs in a 6-month (12-month) period.
3. Average length of time employees remain in the same job, by job class.
4. Extent to which class specifications identify clear career progression within each class (review of class specifications).

Source: S.J. Mushkin, F.H. Sandifer, and C. Warren, *Assessing Personnel Management: Objectives and Performance Indicators*, Public Services Laboratory, Georgetown University, Washington, D.C., 1977.

5. Number and percentage of employees who complain about lack of advancement to selected personnel managers.

C. Subobjective: To identify the knowledges, skills, and abilities needed to perform each kind and level of job for recruitment, training, and pay purposes.

Indicators

1. Percentage of job class specifications used as a basis for personnel actions (recruitment, training, pay review).
2. Number of employees taking courses to develop specified skills.
3. Percentage of employees trained in specific skills who report use of new skills on job.
4. Measured success in terms of output or performance of training programs that train for knowledge, skills, and abilities identified in job classifications (see Employee Development, subobjective B).

D. Subobjective: To provide an accurate basis for review, analysis, and evaluation of organization, functions, work flow, work methods, and staff/equipment utilization.

Indicators

1. Number of instances in last 6 months (12 months) in which job descriptions have been used as data sources in management analyses of organizations, programs, or functions.
2. Number of instances in last 6 months (12 months) in which management analysis led to changes in job classifications.

II. Recruitment and Selection

A. Subobjective: To hire employees in order to reach and maintain a staffing level (numbers and qualifications) sufficient to meet public service requirements.

Indicators

1. Percentage of agency requests met within specified time.
2. Average period of time budgeted jobs remain vacant after recruitment request has been made.
3. Number of "successful" employees selected, as measured by:
   a. Production data
      Quality
      Quantity
   b. Job knowledge tests
   c. Supervisory or peer ratings

4. Cost and percentage of personnel staff engaged in recruitment and selection per new hire.
5. Percentage of new employees who fail probation.
6. Percentage of new employees who voluntarily leave within the first 12 months.
7. Percentage of new employees who successfully complete the first 12 months.
8. Percentage of new employees who earn promotions within the first 18 months (24 months).

B. Subobjective: To facilitate the hiring of well-qualified employees by ensuring that potential candidates have the opportunity of being considered for employment.

Indicators

1. Length of time between examinations.
2. Number and accessibility of examination sites (average travel time for selected examinees, by grade level).
3. Extent to which announcements of examinations are publicized.
4. Number of complaints concerning hours and days in which examinations are given.

III. Compensation, Including Fringe Benefits

A. Subobjective: To motivate employees to maintain a high level of performance through adequate and equitable compensation.

Indicators

1. Comparison of pay in the government for selected occupations (total salary and value of fringe benefits) with that of other public and private employers in the labor market.
2. Comparison of pay for different occupations in selected agencies or departments (total remuneration, as above).
3. Number and percentage of employees working under incentive pay plans.
4. Number and percentage of employees receiving pay increases for superior performance.

IV. Performance Appraisals and Promotion, Firing, and Transfers

A. Subobjective: To identify (for employees, supervisors, and managers) specific employee performance weaknesses to be corrected and strengths to be enhanced and best utilized.

Indicators

1. Percentage of employees whose performance is evaluated periodically against established standards or objectives.

2. Percentage of performance appraisals that directly prompt the following types of actions:
   a. Promotions
   b. Terminations
   c. Reassignments
   d. Step increases or bonus pay
   e. Reclassifications
   f. Training and development
3. Number and percentage of jobs that lend themselves to output measurement for evaluation purposes.
4. Number and percentage of jobs in which supervisory (or peer) review suggests superior performance to achieve unit mission.

B. Subobjective: To encourage employees to strive for higher performance and overall excellence.

Indicators

1. Types of merit programs offered by the government which formally recognize superior performance.
2. Number of employee proposals (innovations, inventions, suggestions) considered by supervisors, and percentage of employees given recognition for proposals.

V. Employee Development

A. Subobjective: To ensure that employees have and maintain the skills and attitudes needed to perform their jobs.

Indicators

1. Number and percentage of employees who:
   a. Understand agency mission and their role in that mission (requires instrumentation)
   b. Have participated in education or training programs, academic or vocational, during the past 12 months
2. Number and types of sponsored training and development programs provided.
3. Proportion of employees, by department and agency, offered (or eligible for) training and development programs.
4. Changes in average test scores of examinations given at the completion of training programs or examinations given for promotion purposes.
5. Changes in available output data or performance measurements (by individual or work unit) following the completion of training programs.
6. Changes (decline or increase) in average test scores of new employees on entrance examinations during the past year (2 years).

7. Percentage of senior positions filled from within, and percentage by new hires.

B. Subobjective: To improve opportunities for advancement (see Classification and Staffing, subobjective B).

VI Employee-Employer Relations

A. Subobjective: To enhance job satisfaction and motivation of employees. (Numerous job satisfaction and need-achievement measures are available, particularly through employee surveys, for example, University of Michigan, *Measures of Occupational Attitudes*.)

Indicators

1. Job turnover rates, by major occupation.
2. Absenteeism rates—average days lost from work.
3. Accident rates on the job, by major occupation.
4. Job satisfaction and work self-fulfillment and self-esteem measurement.

B. Subobjective: To improve workforce effectiveness through (a) recognition of organizations or unions chosen by employees to represent them and (b) negotiating with employees collectively through their bargaining units.

Indicators

1. Number of separate bargaining units, number of employees per unit.
2. Average length of time to negotiate labor agreements, selected bargaining units.
3. Number of employee grievances.
4. Average length of time required to resolve grievances.
5. Number of employees covered by productivity bargaining contract provisions.
6. Percentage of negotiated labor agreements that contain productivity provisions.
7. Number of labor negotiations that include productivity as a bargaining issue.

VII. EEO-Affirmative Action

A. Subobjective: To increase the responsiveness of government through attainment of a more nearly representative workforce.

Indicators

1. Number and percentage of minority group members in workforce compared with population of the jurisdiction (population of the employment region).

2. Number and frequency of EEO complaints and appeals.
3. Changes during a specified period in the proportion of management-level positions held by target group members.
4. Changes in the distribution of target group members among pay grades and classifications.
5. Changes in the percentage of new hirings of target group members.
6. Changes in the number of promotions obtained by target group members.
7. Changes in the percentage of market group employees subjected to adverse personnel actions.
8. Response of nonminority members to EEO-Affirmative Action programs.

4

The Costs of Personnel Management

Any discussion of the productivity, or performance, of personnel management would be seriously deficient if it failed to address the costs of personnel management activities and of alternative methods of achieving the desired levels of effectiveness in personnel management. As we have indicated previously, productivity in essence means effectiveness in relation to costs.

Unfortunately, very little information is readily available about the costs of personnel management in any given local government or across local governments generally. Accounting practices and organizational structures differ greatly among cities. Moreover, what is normally included in the category "personnel" excludes some of the most important costs of personnel management in the governments.

The question is sometimes posed: Why the concern about personnel management when the total budget for the personnel department is only a small fraction of city outlays? One official posed the question more specifically: "The police department's budget is $10 million this year, while the personnel department spends $200,000. Why should the mayor spend his scarce time on personnel management?" There are a couple convincing answers:

1. The personnel department's budget is only the visible tip of personnel management costs. There is far more involved in personnel management than the fairly limited activities that are paid for in the personnel department budget.
2. Personnel management has a lot to do with the efficiency and effectiveness of the police services purchased with that department's $10 million budget.

One of the misconceptions that we have addressed before in this book is the idea that the central personnel agency and its activities make up the totality of personnel management. Every manager in a government organization is likely to be mainly a personnel manager. The cost of that portion of a manager's time which is devoted to personnel management is an important part of the costs of personnel management.

This chapter is an attempt to at least partially close the gap in knowledge and understanding about personnel management costs. The first part of the chapter reports what generally is known about these costs across cities (primarily personnel agency costs). The second part sets forth a model for analyzing the costs of personnel management as a part of assessing such management decisions.

Existing Data on Costs of Personnel Management

Deficiencies in existing statistical compilations of personnel management costs stand in the way of analyses of intercity differences and even prevent the identification of issues. Intercity differences which appear to be large may be mere statistical artifacts. In general, the deficiencies that need to be repaired are the lack of uniformity in definition of scope, lack of uniformity in coverage, inadequacies in reporting information, and lack of uniformity in city accounting. As a start toward overcoming these deficiencies, there clearly must be a careful assessment of existing nationwide data on state and city personnel from the decennial census, the Census of Governments, the U.S. Bureau of Labor Statistics, and Internal Revenue data. Such an assessment is far beyond the scope of this study.

Most local governments have multiagency responsibilities for personnel but in different combinations. Costs are incurred by operating agencies for personnel work, but the extent of their personnel responsibilities varies widely. Furthermore, the budgets of many cities' personnel departments are not allocated for specific functions, and different accounting systems lead to disparate categorization of functions even in cities where costs are broken down and isolated. Figure 4-1 shows that for one local government, San Diego County, a number of central government agencies are involved in carrying out aspects of personnel functions outside of the Civil Service Commission and personnel department.

Some cities, particularly, the smaller ones, do not have separate budgets for the personnel department. In many of these cities, the personnel budget is included with that of the finance, administration, or accounting departments. In larger cities, consolidations of the personnel functions at the center have often met with opposition despite the known history of patchwork responses to new circumstances, such as affirmative action for women or CETA programs. San Diego County is far from atypical.

There also is the very significant cost of supervisory and managerial time devoted to personnel management. Generally, these costs are likely to grow with the size of the staff being supervised. However, there are no reliable data on these costs. With reasonable effort, usable estimates across jurisdictions could be developed.

The International Personnel Management Association (IPMA) collects some intercity data on personnel management costs.[1] These data, however, cover only the budgets of specifically designated personnel agencies. Thus they identify only one piece of cities' personnel management costs. The governments division of the U.S. Bureau of the Census, the federal agency that regularly collects and compiles financial and employment data on state and local governments, does not collect personnel management information.

IPMA's survey data for cities reporting show total personnel agency budgets of $42.6 million in 1976, or an average of $123 per city employee covered by

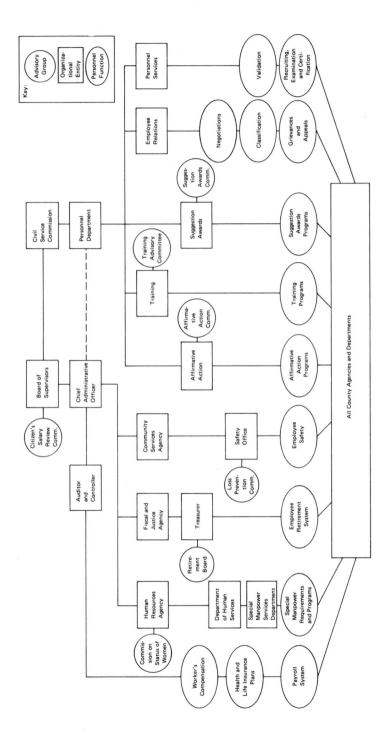

Figure 4-1. Personnel Relationships.

Source: State of California, County of San Diego, Office of Program Evaluation, Evaluation of San Diego County Personnel Policies, San Diego, California, 1976.

the personnel agencies. Approximately 74 percent of the total personnel agency budgets was accounted for by the salaries of personnel agency staffs.

To put this kind of information in perspective, it is useful to reexamine figure 4-1. In many cities, the functions encompassed in the personnel budget as reported to the IPMA would be, at most, only those under the Civil Service Commission, or only the right half of figure 4-1. Such other governmentwide personnel functions as health and life insurance plans, the retirement system, payroll, and employee safety are excluded, as well as whatever personnel functions have been decentralized to operating departments.

Despite the obvious limitations of the IPMA data, it is worthwhile to examine them for significant features. For example, in table 4-1, the third column (total personnel budget per employee covered) gives an indication of economies of scale in the work of personnel agencies. The average personnel agency budget per employee covered is considerably higher for smaller cities than for middle-sized cities and higher for middle-sized cities than for large cities.[2] We have applied correlation and regression analysis to the IPMA data to determine how personnel agency costs relate to city size. For these analyses, 98 cities were included; the very largest few and the very small were left out. The simple correlation coefficient was computed between personnel agency budgets and city populations across the 98 remaining cities. The correlation coefficient was significantly positive, at +.86. The relationship is so strong that even when the effects of the numbers of employees covered and the total city budgets are controlled for, the relationship between personnel agency budget and city population still is significantly larger than zero.[3]

The data reported indicate that personnel agency budgets are related to city size.[4] The regression coefficient relating personnel agency budgets to population implies an elasticity of .62, which means that for every 1 percent increase in city population, the personnel agency budget increases by $\frac{6}{10}$ of 1 percent, or it increases less than proportionately to population. The elasticity coefficient suggests economies of scale. Another approach to estimating whether there are economies of scale in personnel agency costs is to eliminate the population variable from both sides of the regression equation and reestimate it. When this is done, the personnel agency budget per capita is significantly negatively related to the number of employees covered by the personnel system, controlling for other influences, such as per capita income level and total governmental expenditures. This reconfirms the hypothesis that there are economies of scale in personnel agency operations, at least as suggested by the IPMA data.

There are, however, some difficulties with the simple economies-of-scale interpretation previously described. Specifically, there is a good chance that the economies of scale are overstated for the larger cities in the IPMA survey sample. Generally, the large cities are likely to decentralize to operating departments some responsibilities that in small- and middle-sized cities are performed by the central personnel agency. This would mean that the personnel agency

Table 4-1
Total Budget and Salaries of Public Personnel Agencies

	Total Budget (in thousands)	Total Salaries (in thousands)	Total Personnel Budget per Employee Covered	Total Personnel Agency Salary Budget per Employee Covered	Personnel Agency Salaries as Percentage of Total City Employee Payroll[a]
All cities in IPMA study[b]	$42,558[c]	$31,535[c]	$123	$ 91	—
Cities above 500,000 population[b]	12,049	8,578	110	78	0.5%
Cities 100,000-500,000 population	22,801	17,815	124	97	0.8
Cities below 100,000 population	7,243	5,504	148	112	n.a.
Six-city average (mean)	403	257	188	120	0.9
Dayton[d]	376	269	123	88	0.7
Lakewood	201	125	334	201	1.6
Nashville-Davidson	n.a.	n.a.	n.a.	n.a.	n.a.
St. Paul	607	479	140	110	1.0
Savannah	167	91	105	57	0.7
Scottsdale	482	124	556	143	1.6
Tacoma	585	455	239	186	1.0
Worcester	n.a.	n.a.	n.a.	n.a.	n.a.

Source: International Personnel Management Association, *Budgets, Staffs, and Pay Rates of Public Personnel Agencies, 1976,* Chicago, Illinois, 1976; U.S. Bureau of the Census, *City Government Finances in 1975-76,* Series GF76, No. 4, Table 5, U.S. Government Printing Office, Washington, D.C., 1977.

[a]Personnel agency salaries, both professional and clerical, of cities in IPMA study as percentage of total city expenditure for labor services (from Bureau of the Census government finances data).

[b]Los Angeles excluded because total budget includes workers' compensation claim and medical payments, health insurance subsidy, and dental insurance subsidy.

[c]Totals do not add due to rounding.

[d]Data from 1974 IPMA study.

budget figures probably are not nearly as comparable between the very large cities and the other cities in the IPMA survey. This feature seems to be illustrated by data that IPMA has reported on the numbers of city departments with internal personnel divisions. For 15 cities with populations over 500,000, four or five departments per city have internal personnel sections. In contrast, 68 cities in the 100,000 to 500,000 population range have a total of only 43 departments among them that have internal personnel staffs—less than one per city.

The last column of table 4-1 shows the relationship between salaries for personnel agency staffs and total budgeted payrolls. On average, the salaries of personnel agency staffs comprise less than 1 percent of total city salary costs.

Table 4-2 displays a different breakdown of the IPMA survey data on municipal personnel agency costs. Across all cities surveyed, the most substantial personnel agency costs can be attributed to four core areas of responsibility: classification and pay administration; recruitment, examination, and placement; administration of benefits and services; and labor relations. In the same way that the table 4-1 data cannot give us an accurate indication of personnel management costs (showing personnel *agency* costs instead), these data cannot define reliably the most important, costly, or time-consuming aspects of municipal personnel management—they show only how the personnel agencies' costs are spread among areas of responsibility. Many cities have separate offices of labor-management relations, Affirmative Action, and other functions that would not be reflected at all in these data.

In summary, the IPMA survey data are valuable because they are the only reasonably comparable intercity information available on any significant part of personnel management in city governments. However, these data raise as many questions as they answer. For instance, are there really economies of scale in municipal personnel management, or do the apparent economies result from decentralization of major personnel management functions in larger cities? The kinds of simple analyses and interpretations we have applied to the IPMA survey data give a hint of the kinds of important policy-related information that could be produced with better data.

IPMA Data on Eight Project Cities

For the medium-sized cities included in our eight-city study, some data are available from the IPMA survey, but the information is reported for only six of the cities.[5] The average personnel agency budget per city employee covered for the six cities is considerably higher than the average for all cities reported (table 4-1). Scottsdale and Lakewood, both of which have fairly small populations and small numbers of city employees relative to other cities, had the highest figures for personnel agency budgets per city employee. On the other hand, Savannah, which also is a relatively small city, had the smallest personnel

Table 4-2
Percent Distribution of Personnel Agency Expenditures by Personnel Function (1976 IPMA Study)

	Classification and Pay Administration	Recruitment, Examination, Placement	Training	Service Rating Plan	Administration of Benefits and Services	Personnel Research	Labor Relations	Other Activities
All cities surveyed (median)	10%	25%	5%	2%	14%	5%	10%	12%
Cities above 500,000 population (median)	14	33	7	1	19	3	5	22
Cities 100,000-500,000 population (median)	14	29	6	2	11	5	10	16
Cities below 100,000 population (median)	10	25	5	3	10	5	10	12
Eight-city average[a]	12	20	10	1	21	5	13	23
Dayton[b]	23	—[c]	25	0	4	4	23	21
Lakewood	20	30	7	3	11	4	12	13
St. Paul	9	38	6	2	8	3	9	25
Savannah	10	14	0	0	18	7	6	45
Scottsdale	3	6	7	n.a.	66	n.a.	n.a.	19
Tacoma	5	30	15	n.a.	18	n.a.	15	17

Source: International Personnel Management Association, *Budgets, Staffs, and Pay Rates of Public Personnel Agencies, 1976*, Chicago, Illinois, 1976; U.S. Bureau of the Census, *Population Estimates and Projections*, Series P-25, May 1977.

[a]Data for Nashville-Davidson and Worcester are not available on a comparable basis.

[b]1974.

[c]Represents zero or rounds to zero.

agency budget per employee. Probably this is the result, at least in part, of regional characteristics of the South. It is interesting to note that the three cities west of St. Paul (Lakewood, Scottsdale, and Tacoma) reported considerably higher personnel agency budgets per employee covered than St. Paul, Dayton, or Savannah.[6] This may be due to more comprehensive coverage of personnel responsibilities by the central personnel agencies in the former group of cities.

Uses of Data on Personnel Management Costs

Why is it important to have better data on the costs of personnel management in cities? For what purposes would the data be used? Let us assume for a moment that the average municipal personnel agency spends $125 per city employee a year. Is this a reasonable amount? If a city personnel agency spends three times this average amount, is it spending too much? There is no answer at present to these or similar questions. And the questions themselves do not really represent the important issues. The "average" city probably has decentralized much of the performance appraisal, employee development, labor relations, affirmative action, and even recruiting and selection functions, especially for particular segments of the city workforce (for example, fire and police). The city with the higher than average costs in the personnel agency may not have decentralized as much of the personnel management responsibility.

Intercity comparisons in effect provide a "standard" for judging the costs of one personnel system against others. If the statistics are adequately compiled, comparisons can be made of costs in cities of similar size, with similar functional responsibilities, similar spending levels, and so forth. When outputs are quantified for personnel management, these cost data can be used to develop productivity indexes of personnel management on a basis of dollars spent. Cost data are not truly useful for comparisons until levels of output–approximations at least–also can be compared.

Toward Quantification of Costs

To improve the type of data so that the scope of personnel work encompasses "personnel management" and is uniformly reported on a recurrent basis requires a substantial effort. Among the steps that would be required are the following:

1. Personnel management functions would have to be clearly defined in such a way that they are acceptable to those in the cities who would be asked to report.
2. "Costs" of personnel management functions would have to be defined so that each component could be identified and costed.

3. Because of the extent of joint management functions, techniques would have to be specified for prorating costs between personnel management and other functions.
4. Decisions would have to be made about the components of personnel management for which data collection would be usefully pursued. Again, each component would need to be defined and procedures outlined for prorating costs where staff perform more than one function.
5. An institutional "home" would have to be found for the statistics gathering that would encourage compliance in the cities with requests for data.
6. Staff for the effort would have to be sufficient to ensure adequate follow-up, editing, tabulation, and analyses of responses from the cities.

The interagency effort headed by the U.S. Civil Service to define components of personnel management and collect agency data on staff time and workload for each of the components marks an important beginning toward a definitional effort.[7] It could well be that equivalent staff years (ESY) are sufficient for intercity comparisons. The ESY indexes, when combined with measures of quality and quantity of personnel management operations, could yield intercity assessments of the productivity of personnel management.

To derive statistics on cost data, the following components of operating and capital costs might be collected:

Salary and wage costs (salaries and wages paid, including the prorated share of salaries of those doing both personnel management and other tasks)

Fringe benefit costs (government costs for fringe benefits, including such benefits as retirement, health insurance, life insurance, education, and sick leave, vacation pay, or disability benefits not included in salaries and wages)

Nonpersonnel operating costs (supplies, contractual services, travel, utilities, communications, rentals, facility maintenance, etc.)

Capital costs (major equipment purchases, property acquisitions, renovations)

Costs of other governments (personnel management services provided by other governments, such as state or county, exclusive of that included under contractual services)

The processes and definitions of the U.S. Bureau of the Census should be reviewed carefully for the guidance they offer for a statistics-gathering effort.

Intercity statistics have important uses, including use for policy formulation and budget allocations. What the statistics help in achieving for an individual city is primarily an identification of problems for scrutiny or analysis. The data become what are often termed "indicators."

Cost Analysis of Personnel Management Decisions

Cost statistics do not take the place of cost analysis. As city governments come to review personnel components of general policies or their personnel systems and ask hard questions about objectives and the functioning or malfunctioning of the systems, questions about costs of optional approaches surface. A government considering consolidation of facilities or program curtailment must assess the personnel consequences of the proposals, methods of alleviating personnel hardships, methods of recruitment and selection, and information about the costs of the current methods and relative costs associated with the proposed changes. If methods of merit pay are under review in a city, and a bonus system, for example, is being considered in lieu of current merit awards, the "costs" will be the add-ons for years of service compared with the amount of the bonus and the numbers of employees selected for such bonuses.

Unlike the standardization of cost items in gathering uniform statistics on expenditures for personnel management, the cost items that are part of cost analysis for program review will vary. The cost-analysis content follows the scope of the program analysis. These can be restricted to such questions as the relative cost of newspaper advertising versus posting vacancy announcements for purposes of recruitment. Or, for instance, the program analysis may involve a fundamental organizational shift from an independent civil service commission to an office of personnel under the mayor, with more personnel responsibility lodged in the agencies. Cost analysis would call for considerable quantification of the many components involved in such a change. Programs under review might require more than simply changing implementation processes and administrative procedures. Large employee training programs might be involved, or changes in retirement or other fringe benefits or in pay structure might be involved. The costs of such fundamental changes would tend to be high, and an effort to estimate these costs would be crucial.

These examples underscore the wide diversity of issues for which cost analyses may be required. Given this wide diversity, what can be said that would provide guidance to those who would undertake a cost analysis?

What Is Cost Analysis?

In this context, *cost analysis* may be defined as a process of compiling and using cost and program data to estimate and project the future costs of one or a number of options for informing decision makers. To achieve the purposes of such analysis, costs for each option must be defined in a uniform way, making every effort to capture total costs. Unless uniformity is achieved, bias is introduced into the cost comparisons.

What Time Period Should Be Covered?

The period over which costs are to be calculated has to be selected in a way that helps in understanding the several options. Often initial-year costs do not represent full costs. Certainly the lessons learned by the cities from the growth of retirement benefit costs underscore the need for long-term projections. Care in cost analysis is needed to ensure that the time period selected is the same for each of the options, so that the comparisons are not distorted.

When costs are being compared over different time periods, to achieve comparability, the appropriate cost to consider is the present value of future costs for a uniform number of years ahead. The standard present value formula is:

$$PV = \sum_{t=0}^{T} \frac{C_t}{(1+r)^t}$$

where PV = present value
  C_t = cost in time period t
  r = discount rate
  T = final year of the time period

Costs incurred in the past that would be unaffected by the options are not relevant to the cost comparisons for purposes of present decision making. Such past costs are "sunk" costs.

Objectives and Generation of Options

The starting point of an analysis is the articulation of the goals or objectives of the program, policy, or budget change under consideration. For example, a change in employee selection procedures may be considered with the goal of ensuring that candidates chosen for positions possess the skills required for successful job performance. Presumably, options would be generated for the accomplishment of each goal.

Steps in an Analysis

The cost analysis starts with the options that are generated to achieve these goals or objectives. The steps to be taken are set forth below to illustrate what is involved in an analysis.

1. Enumerating all the functions and processes which are necessary for the realization of the specified goals and objectives and the options generated. For instance, each agency, division, or department is asked to provide specifications on particular skills needed in all job classifications for which methods of candidate selection are being considered. This step provides the initial basis for identification of information on the major classes of resources needed.
2. Examining the sequence of the processes by setting forth the work flow (or network) involved in each option. This step provides essentially a check on step 1.
3. Determining a method for estimating and analyzing costs, including the development of a cost model. The many factors involved in cost analysis for a major change in personnel management processes or policies point to a systematic methodology for preparing estimates that can be used for each option. The model can economize on time and improve the accuracy of comparisons.
4. Identifying existing cost data sources to be used in the model. Data sources might include organization charts, performance measures or monitoring reports, master plans, budget documents, and expenditure reports.
5. Determining how to structure the cost data. All major categories of resources that would be used in the proposed changes in personnel management must be identified. These categories are generally referred to as *cost elements*. The full list of cost elements comprises the cost-element structure.
6. Determining the major cost elements. In cost analysis of personnel management options, it often will be sufficient to determine the costs involved in staffing the several options. Accordingly, a major step will be to determine the amount of staff time required for the performance of each of the functions or activities called for by the options and the number of full-time equivalent (FTE) employees to which this corresponds. It may be useful to classify functions according to the similarity of process to ensure that all functions are included (for example, determination and specification of skills necessary for new personnel, job design, determination of appropriate salary and promotion tracks). [Support staff (secretarial and clerical) should be assigned as well.]
7. Determining the quantities of each cost element to be considered (for example, if additional employees are required, how many are needed?). This step yields the basic information on the numbers in each cost element.
8. Assigning a cost to each element (if the cost element being used is salaries per FTE, and the salary levels for a specific function are very different, then a weighted average may be applied).
9. For complete cost analysis, determining non-personnel-related operating costs, capital costs, and external or secondary costs. For purposes of estimating, one can often approximate total operating expenditures using a

ratio of total personnel costs to total costs. The underlying assumption is that expenditures for personnel can be used to impute other operating costs, because personnel costs are the largest single expenditure category, and the number of staff determine, in part, how large operating costs will be. Although this assumption cannot be extended logically to capital and external costs, these costs often form only a small part of the total.

10. Estimating the relationship for various cost elements included in the cost model (step 2). Various methods are available to derive these estimates. Regression analysis is often used. The method selected, however, depends on the type of problem and the assumed relationship.

Characteristics of Cost Analysis

Certain characteristics of cost analysis for analytical purposes may be emphasized; for example:

Cost elements are defined in a uniform way to help ensure comparability. In the case of salary levels used as a cost component, questions about such items as vacations, sick leave, retirement costs, and health insurance must be clarified. In practice, it is often feasible to apply a standard "fringe benefit" rate to salaries for estimating purposes.

The aim is to achieve a reasonable accuracy that permits officials to choose among the options. Striving for precision can be both unnecessary and costly in terms of data collection and data analysis.

The *additional* costs that would be incurred by adoption of the particular alternative are the relevant costs.

Both current and future year cost implications of the program choice must be considered. (The number of years to consider will depend on the type of program under scrutiny.)

While many costs can be measured in dollars, estimates of other types of costs in terms of requirements for limited resources must also be included, for example, use of specialized personnel.

Secondary financial effects also need to be considered, whether plus or minus, and whether they affect the jurisdiction's own budget or occur outside the government, perhaps resulting in gains or losses to private businesses or individuals.

Some of the characteristics of costing for analytical purposes perhaps warrant further elaboration here. "Costs" for program analysis are not the same as costs for comparative statistical purpose. As indicated, "sunk" costs are not relevant to a cost analysis. Many costs of personnel functions are costs that fall in the caption, which we here label "for want of a nail, a kingdom is lost." If a large public investment is partially wasted because personnel with sufficient skills to operate machines are neither found nor trained, or if expensive equipment is damaged by lack of motivation or understanding, then the savings in recruitment or training costs that are primary personnel management costs must be set alongside the added costs in equipment. Even the costs of the added risks of an epidemic for failure to use new equipment for waste treatment in cleaning the water might be considered. For lack of trained staff, a "kingdom is lost."

Secondary costs also include costs incurred by other jurisdictions and private industry. It is customary in government to consider only the costs that become a claim on the city's own current budget. But in personnel management, the blinders that limit the scope of factors considered may, for some purposes, work mischief.

For example, a city that raises its pay levels or fringe benefits because of inadequate personnel management may disrupt private firms in the area by pushing up local pay scales, thus impairing the capacity of local firms to compete with those in other cities. Or if pay rates are set so low that only marginal workers are attracted, services may deteriorate and private industry costs go up because of greater waiting or processing time, errors, and delays in issuance of licenses and permits. In a number of cases, the state or federal government, rather than the city, incur the costs. The extent of cost shifting should be known. It may well be that the city will be guided by its own cost impacts, but at least the decisions will be made with a fuller view of the total costs associated with the change.

Cost Elements for Cost Analysis

As described in the preceding discussion, analysis requires the determination of uniform cost elements for all options under review. Costs may be categorized in various ways, but it is important to try to take account of total added costs, some of which may not be readily apparent. Figure 4-2 illustrates one useful way of categorizing and displaying the cost elements.

Direct operating costs include both personnel costs (for example, salaries and fringe benefits) and nonpersonnel operating costs (for example, supplies, equipment, space rental, and contract services). For many analytical efforts, the identification of payroll costs provides a good starting point for the analysis. Again, personnel is the largest single expenditure category and may be used to approximate other operating costs. One item that should be approximated, but frequently is ignored, is the cost of managers' and supervisors' time engaged in relevant personnel management activities.

Additional capital costs include major equipment purchases and any construction required to implement a program option.

Type of Cost for Each Option	Initial Year	+1	+2	+3	+4	Total 5-Year Cost
Main cost categories						
Direct costs						
Indirect (or secondary costs)						
Direct operating costs						
☐ Option I						
II						
III						
Added capital costs						
☐ Option I						
II						
III						
Indirect (or secondary) costs to city (if any)						
☐ Option I Loss of employee time						
II Loss of employee time for supervisors doing training						
III						
Costs of other governments (if any)						
☐ Option I Added costs to community colleges						
II						
III						
Private costs						
☐ Option I Cost of transportation to place of training						
II						
III						
Total						
Total costs						
☐ Option I						
II						
III						

Note: Summarize the estimated costs of each option over, for example, a 5-year period.

Figure 4-2. Statement of Estimated Costs: Initial Year and Several Out-Years.

Indirect costs to city represent costs that are not usually counted in the budgeting or accounting systems but nevertheless are costs in resources used. Examples are the value of space in a city-owned facility or the value of city employee time for which no additional salary costs are incurred.

Costs of other governments represent costs (both monetary and imputed values) that fall on other governmental jurisdictions. Examples are the state government's costs for a modification in Civil Service provisions to effect a change in personnel management in the cities or costs to the state of retirement benefits paid to community employees under state law.

Private costs include the costs (both monetary and imputed value) that individuals and industry incur as a consequence of city personnel management actions. Examples might include increased labor costs, as mentioned earlier.

Example

To illustrate cost analysis, let us assume that a change is being considered in employee training. Several options are being considered, including:

1. Training on behalf of the government in the local community college.
2. Training functions left in the agencies as on-the-job training.
3. Training by the personnel department.

In developing the costs, it is useful to consider each of the three options separately, beginning with the question: What are the processes involved? For example, without intending in any way a comprehensive examination, the processes associated with training by the personnel department might be specified as shown in the list below (assuming purposes of training are already defined and curriculum and training materials are "on shelf"). Cost considerations are involved in each of these processes.

Agency identification of trainees

Agency transmission of selections to personnel department

Personnel department decision on numbers of trainees

Personnel department designation of trainers

Personnel department designation of training sites

Personnel department designation of training dates

Carrying out of training

Evaluation of training

Assuming that the numbers of employees to be trained are about the same under each option, what are the cost differences? Let us assume that the curriculum and training materials are available, so that development costs for these have already been incurred (that is, they are "sunk" costs), and that these costs are uniformly available for each of the options.

As indicated in the earlier discussion of steps of analysis, the main tasks are to:

1. Determine the appropriate unit of measurement for each of the types of costs elements.
2. Analyze the relationships that define the required number of units of each cost element.
3. Analyze the relationships determining unit costs.

An initial task is to define the units of cost measurement. The main cost element is direct costs of salaries (salaries of trainers and teachers). If the training is contracted out to a local community college, contractual costs or tuition would be included as an operating expense. Fringe-benefit costs would be counted, as well as supply and material costs, space rental (or an imputed value of these rentals as an indirect cost), telephone, and equipment costs.

Direct personnel costs would be established in terms of the number and grade levels of the employees responsible for training. Some prorated share of personnel department administrative costs might be included, but a considerable part of those costs represent "sunk" costs, or "overhead," that do not vary from option to option. Additionally, the costs associated with identifying trainees and transmitting the selection to the personnel department, at least in this example, probably are fixed costs—the same for all the options.

An important category of training costs is the indirect cost of time lost from productive work, including the salaries and fringe benefits of employees for time spent in training. For the options calling for agency training, there is also the cost of the on-the-job trainer's time lost from other work. For all options, there is the overtime or other arrangements for performing the work of the employees who are in training and the costs of delays in getting work done while employees are in training. Other indirect costs might be the participant's costs of travel to training sites above the normal costs of travel to and from work.

What are the numbers of units required of each cost component? The model approximating the relationship between number of employees to be trained and personnel resources required for the training draws essentially on the description of the several options. The number of trainers, for example, is a function of the number of employees to be trained. If outside facilities are used, such as a community college, the initial question is the facilities available. It could be that additional teachers would be required, or, under some circumstances, the existing teaching services may be sufficient and the marginal costs may be small for the projected number of enrollees or trainees.

A useful technique for estimating the number of units required is a regression analysis. In this example, the number of trainers is shown as dependent on (a function of) the number of trainees. For example, figure 4-3 shows the relationship

$$T = f(tr)$$

where T = number of trainers
tr = number of trainees

What are the unit costs likely to be? In the example used here, what are the salary and fringe benefits of a trainer? Past experience must be drawn upon to structure the future unit-cost relationships.

Examining the average salary of trainers over the past period may suggest an outlay of $18,000 per trainer, including salary and government fringe-benefit contributions. Personal service outlays have risen, past experience indicates, by 9 percent per year, of which 3 percent is the assumed correspondence with private productivity increases and 6 percent the cost of living increase. Based on these experiences, the cost-estimating relationship may be expressed in this way:

$$P_s = \$18,000 \, (1 + .09)t$$

where P_s = average salary plus city contributions toward fringe benefits
t = time elapsing

The number of units of cost (for example, number of trainers) and the cost per unit are combined to derive the total cost. The cost equation is $T \cdot P_s$, or number of trainers times the average salary and fringe benefits per trainer.

The development of a cost model appropriate for a particular personnel management problem requires a real understanding of the way or ways in which the cost model is to be used. Often it is necessary to experiment with different models before a satisfactory one is found that can capture with maximum simplicity the essential cost variations. Model building for costing purposes is an art as much as a science.

However, it must be emphasized that cost analysis can be, and often is, carried out with what appears to be a far greater measure of precision than the circumstances warrant.

The cost analysis of options is intended to provide estimates of the relative costs of some optional processes or policies, so that when they are combined with estimates of effectiveness, choices can be made by public officials with a greater amount of information. In making comparisons, it frequently is useful

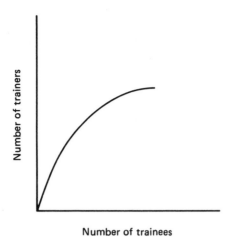

Figure 4-3. Number of Trainers Dependent on Number of Trainees

to determine a "base case" of the total costs involved, from which the incremental costs of changes in practices or policies can be judged. The cost model helps answer "what if" questions in a way that yields meaningful and yet not exact cost comparisons. The cost worksheet (figure 4-2) helps to summarize the estimates derived.

Notes

1. *Budgets, Staffs, and Pay Rates of Public Personnel Agencies, 1976*, International Personnel Management Association, survey of members, Chicago, 1976.

2. While data for the city of Los Angeles were reported by IPMA, they have been excluded from our tabulations because they include costs that are not comparable to the other cities in the sample.

3. The equation estimated is:

$$PERSBUDG = 31038.4 + .948 \, CITYPOP + 31.27 \, EMPLCOV + 27.18 \, EXPEND$$
$$(4.42) \qquad\qquad (2.15)^* \qquad\qquad (.31)$$

$$\overline{R}^2 = .75 \quad F = 95.9\dagger$$

where t ratios are in parentheses, $\dagger$ indicates significance at .01 level, and * indicates significance at the .05 level. The variable definitions are PERSBUDG, total personnel agency budget; CITYPOP, city population; EMPLCOV, number of employees covered by the personnel agency; and EXPEND, city government expenditures per capita. The coefficient on city population implies that for every additional resident in a city, the personnel agency budget increases by $.95. The elasticity, calculated at the mean values, implies that a 1 percent increase in city population is associated with a .62 percent increase in personnel agency budget.

4. City population is likely not as direct a determining factor as would appear on surface examination. Rather, the probable relationship is that larger populations require more services, necessitating a larger city workforce, which in turn requires the services of a relatively larger personnel agency budget.

5. Conceptually it would be desirable to relate personnel management costs (even partial costs, such as the personnel agency budget per employee covered) to measures of personnel management effectiveness. One might reasonably attempt to relate the personnel agency budget per employee with the perceived impact of personnel management components on city productivity actions, as derived in our eight-city survey. However, our sample of eight cities was too small for statistical inferences of such a relationship based on correlation or regression analysis.

6. Skillfully designed survey instruments, applied to an appropriately stratified sample of local government managerial employees and officials, probably could determine enough about managers' time devoted to personnel management functions to allow for suggesting a standard proration factor.

7. J.D.R. Cole and A.S. Udler, "Productivity and Personnel," *Civil Service Journal* 17(2):23 (October-December 1976).

5 Summary Comments on Personnel Management and Government Productivity

That there is a strong and important relationship between personnel management in a city government and that government's productivity should surprise no one. Productivity is primarily determined by the performance of the government's workers, and their performance is in large measure conditioned by the personnel management policies, procedures, and practices. Earlier, we described how a number of management officials and employees in eight cities perceive the relationship between the various elements of personnel management and some of their cities' specific productivity-improvement efforts. Those survey results are useful in helping to define many of the features of the productivity-personnel management relationship.

In the course of this and related projects, we have spent a great deal of time reviewing available literature that is pertinent to the subjects of personnel management and productivity. Included are studies and reports on worker motivation, job satisfaction, productivity and performance measurement, job design/redesign/enrichment, organizational analysis, employee performance evaluation, incentive structures, productivity bargaining, and many other topics. In addition, much time has been devoted to talking to and corresponding with knowledgeable people from a wide range of disciplines and backgrounds—a variety of individuals who contributed many valuable ideas, suggestions, and conclusions. There is clear agreement that personnel management generally and specific components of personnel management have a critical impact on the productivity of governments.

Elsewhere in this book, we discuss the three basic objectives of personnel management in a city government: (1) to provide the human resources required for effective and efficient delivery of needed services to the public, (2) to assure the responsiveness and responsibility of government workers to the citizenry, and (3) to provide leadership in maintaining and improving the quality of working life. Many would argue that these three objectives are causally related, that, for example, ensuring the responsiveness and responsibility of workers to the citizens (2) contributes to effective and efficient delivery of services (1), and that improving the quality of working life and job satisfaction of government workers (3) will lead to both greater effectiveness and efficiency and improved worker responsibility. There are many others, however, who would argue that in practice cities' efforts to achieve the objectives are in conflict with one another. They would contend, for instance, that Affirmative Action programs in the cities frequently impair effectiveness and efficiency,

77

or that efforts to improve government workers' job satisfaction often result in diminished organizational accountability and in an overall decline in efficiency. Neither group is entirely right or entirely wrong. There definitely is a strong connection between the three objectives, a kind of constructive tension that mandates a balanced approach to achieving all three of them. Concentration on efficiency of government service delivery as the sole objective of personnel management—to the exclusion of other equally important objectives—may result in an actual decline in performance, caused by dissatisfied and insecure workers. The primary job of management in a government—the personnel management job—is to develop and implement a workable, integrated, and sufficiently flexible approach to accomplishing the three basic objectives collectively.

What do we know about the relative importance of the various aspects of personnel management programs and practices on governmental performance and productivity? Sufficient information is available to make a series of qualitative observations. In presenting these observations, we will reference some of the results from the eight-city survey as either illustrative or supportive of the points made. It should be noted, however, that the eight-city survey was not designed to produce generalizations about U.S. cities as a group, or even about medium-sized cities. The survey cities were not chosen randomly for study, nor were the respondents within each city selected at random. On the other hand, this does not mean that the survey results are necessarily atypical. While the eight cities do not represent a random sample of medium-sized cities, neither are they wholly uncharacteristic of that universe. In fact, the eight cities appear to be in the vanguard in attempting to deal with and resolve managerial problems and inefficiencies. We would expect the survey results to be of considerable relevance to most other cities.

Job Satisfaction, Motivation, and Productivity

For quite some time, there has been considerable interest in enhancing the satisfaction of workers about their jobs. The late 1960s and early 1970s particularly saw a burgeoning of interest in job satisfaction. The general theory behind many of the job-satisfaction efforts was that if workers are more satisfied with their jobs, they will be better motivated and therefore more productive. A recent NSF-financed study, *Work, Productivity, and Job Satisfaction* (Katzell et al., 1975), deals with many of the issues involved. This report groups workers into four possible categories:

1. Satisfied and highly motivated
2. Satisfied and weakly motivated
3. Dissatisfied and highly motivated
4. Dissatisfied and weakly motivated

Forging the link between work satisfaction and productivity depends critically on increasing the size of the first of the four groups—people who are both satisfied *and* highly motivated.[1]

The authors note that "the specific task of mobilizing human resources to maximize quality of working life and economic performance at the same time is largely a matter of sound managerial practices. . . . "[2] In summarizing their findings, they present a list of six "critical ingredients of systems which may attain the desired dual objective of higher productivity and job satisfaction." Those ingredients are:

a. Financial compensation of workers must be linked to their performance and to productivity gains.

b. Workers and work must be matched so as to create a work situation which workers will see as capable of meeting their needs and expectations, and where they will have the capabilities and resources to be successful.

c. For workers who desire it, their work should provide opportunity for full use of their abilities, making a meaningful contribution, having challenging and diversified duties, and being responsible for others.

d. Workers at all levels must have inputs to plans and decisions affecting their jobs and working lives.

e. Appropriate resources, including work methods and equipment, must be provided to facilitate workers' performance and minimize obstacles to carrying out their jobs.

f. Adequate "hygiene" conditions must exist, including competent and considerate supervision, fair pay and fringe benefits, job security, good working conditions, and sound employee relations.[3]

The Katzell report does not deal with the responsiveness and responsibility of government workers to the citizens as an explicit objective, nor does it present their findings and conclusions specifically in terms of improved personnel management policies and practices. The report does note, however, that "effecting those outcomes [job satisfaction and productivity] is primarily managerial in character, more particularly the management of human resources."[4]

The Vital Elements of Personnel Management

Two of the most important facets of personnel management in a government in terms of performance or productivity are the rather loosely defined sets of activities we call employee-employer relations and supervision. They are unlike the fairly discrete, although related, components of personnel management which this book mainly has discussed, and they will be addressed separately at the end of this chapter. Before that, however, we shall deal with a series of other vital elements in the personnel management framework of the government that have a substantial bearing on the productivity of the government's employees and the overall performance of the government organization. These include employee classification, compensation, performance appraisal, selection, employee development, and collective bargaining.

Classification

Most governments and other organizations of the size we have dealt with in this project have some type of formal position or employee classification system or plan. It provides the underlying structural and information base for many personnel-related decisions, such as staff allocation, compensation, recruitment, promotions, and transfers. Too often, however, it is viewed as something pure and inviolable, as if it were unrelated to the rest of personnel management and to the necessarily changing nature of government work and work methods. This kind of viewpoint produces organizational anachronisms and rigidities that defeat the purposes of classification, impair the ability of managers to manage, and undermine efforts to raise productivity. Perhaps the most popularly known example comes not from government, but from the railroad industry. It took many years and much bargaining with the union for the railroads to finally do away with the fireman job classification and the concomitant requirement for firemen on all trains—long after the switch to diesel and electric locomotives. Other examples, both public and private, abound. In some municipalities, for instance, the governments' building maintenance workers have been classified as carpenters, even though the day had long passed when carpentry skills were required. The result is the hiring of union-certified carpenters at perhaps twice the going salary for regular maintenance personnel.

These are cases in which workforce utilization is subservient to and determined by rigid and outdated classification plans. Through a gradual process, usually over a period of many years, the correct order of things has gotten reversed. The classification plan should be dependent upon, and reflective of, the current workforce, the way it is deployed, and requirements for productivity improvement.

The results of the eight-city survey section on classification emphasize the "procedures for getting positions classified properly." The respondents perceived those procedures as impediments to their cities' productivity actions. As mentioned in chapter 2, the negative response may have been conditioned somewhat by the customary friction between managers and the personnel department staff over who should determine how a position should be classified. It also may have resulted from managers' frustration at trying to upgrade classifications (with resulting higher salary levels) in order to attract and retain high-quality personnel. In any case, however, the survey results appear to reflect the general difficulty in getting the classification system to bear a reasonable relationship to what the managerial respondents perceive the real world to be—that is, the difficulty of getting positions classified on the basis of what the job holders actually do, the outputs they produce, and how they contribute to the overall organization's achievement of its goals.

While there is the real problem of rigidities and outdatedness in many local governments' classification systems, there is also an equally serious problem of ensuring the integrity of the classification process. It is not at all unusual for the personnel department to find itself under pressure from both government managers and employee unions to upgrade position classifications. Both groups are pursuing interests that are fundamentally legitimate, but the use of the classification system to achieve those interests means ignoring existing problems in personnel management and creating future problems. The unions are looking for higher salaries for city workers overall, and the general upgrading of position classifications would produce this result. Managers, as indicated before, frequently are trying to find a way of rewarding their best employees, generally workers who have reached the top of the pay range for their particular job classifications and for whom the existing personnel management structure offers no additional rewards. In either case, the existing classification system is not the appropriate route to take. For the unions, negotiation of pay rates with management is the proper method. For the frustrated managers and supervisors, what is required is to face up to and correct the problems of the city's performance incentives, which probably will involve at the minimum correcting the deficiencies in performance appraisal, compensation, *and* classification.

Classification must be based on effective job analysis. For any given job, this means a rigorous examination of what the job entails, what the duties and responsibilities are, what the job holder must produce, and the relative value of those products to the organization. Regardless of how the particular classification plan or system is structured, the thoroughness and accuracy of job analysis is what makes it work or not work. Classifications must also be current; each position must be reevaluated regularly to determine whether it is classified properly.[5]

Compensation

Compensation—the pay and fringe benefits of government workers—has at least two critical roles to fulfill in the government organization:

1. To provide an adequate level of pay and benefits so that employees are not dissatisfied or insecure, which can be called the "hygiene" role[6]
2. To provide incentives and rewards for superior employee performance, which can be called the motivator role

There has been a great deal of research and debate over what kind—and how much—of an effect compensation has on employees' motivation and performance. In terms of Maslow's "hierarchy of needs," compensation basically is among the lower order of worker needs, which, once secured, no longer serve as motivating forces.[7] However, Maslow and others have attributed great importance to workers' needs for recognition, self-esteem, and peer group status. Most research has been incapable of distinguishing clearly between the monetary and psychological (recognitional) values of increases in compensation.

For some workers, motivation stems at least in part from a desire to achieve greater financial rewards, so that performance pay increases can serve as powerful incentives to and reinforcers of performance. For others, the financial value of pay increases above a basic security (hygiene) level serves no motivating purpose, but the recognition that a pay increase represents may serve as a performance incentive. Finally, there are workers for whom compensation likely has no motivating effect, either in terms of the monetary or recognitional values. Satisfied with their financial situation and their peer group status, these workers may be motivated solely by other (so-called self-actualization) factors, such as greater job-related challenge or greater freedom to pursue specific interests.

If compensation has the capability of serving as an incentive or motivator for employees to perform well and as a reinforcer of superior performance, such capability is denied by the compensation practices of many local governments. In fact, the opposite effect may be achieved; that is, the compensation practices may serve as disincentives to performance and reinforce only average performance by employees. The employees who have the incentive to perform well are mainly those whose motivation derives totally from factors other than compensation. Often so-called merit systems end up rewarding just about everyone in the government who is not totally incompetent and who has served the government for a requisite period of time. To reward everyone is, in effect, to reward no one. Furthermore, to provide merit pay increases to everyone has the same effect as saying that average performance is what the government wants of its employees. Superior performers who might be motivated by compensation will get the message eventually that there is no need to work harder or better—the pay increases will come regardless. Furthermore, it seems likely that the motivated, superior performer will become dissatisfied with his job situation because of the inequity between his compensation and that of others who do the same kinds of work but not as well and yet receive the same pay increases.

In trying to use compensation as a motivator for greater employee effectiveness and efficiency, there are some basic principles which obtain, whether the motivating effect is derived from the monetary value of compensation rewards or from the recognitional value.

Workers must understand and be confident of the relationship between their performance and their compensation.

Workers and management alike must understand and accept the performance criteria that determine rewards.

Rewards must be tied as closely as possible to the worker's performance (that is, rewards must be linked if possible to specific incidents of excellent performance).

Rewards should go only to those who meet or exceed the agreed-upon performance criteria.

In the context of this discussion, it is worthwhile to review the results of the eight-city survey which relate to compensation. These results appear to provide some evidence that the eight cities overall are adequately fulfilling the "hygiene" role of compensation, at least in the view of the managerial officials and employees who were surveyed. Respondents overall did not perceive problems with the two listed compensation factors that best represented the hygiene role:

Salaries and benefits as compared with those of private industry and other public employers

Relationship of pay levels to the quantity, quality, and degree of difficulty of employees' outputs

These two factors appear to have conveyed to respondents the issue of whether city government workers in their cities generally received adequate and appropriate pay and benefits.

In contrast, the three other compensation factors that were listed in the survey instrument related more closely to the motivational or performance-rewards aspects of compensation, and they were perceived, on average, as impeding productivity improvement. They were:

Procedures for establishing or changing pay levels

Procedures for establishing or changing fringe benefits

Policies and procedures for rewarding superior performance (through increased pay or benefits)

The last of these clearly was the most important in the view of survey respondents. A majority of the respondents chose it as the one compensation factor that *could have* provided the greatest support to their cities' productivity actions. Compensation is one of the specific factors that Katzell et al. dealt with directly in their evaluation of policy-related research. Their summary conclusions provide a useful synopsis of what can reasonably be expected of compensation practices, based on the research that has been conducted:[8]

1. Not surprisingly, the more workers are paid, the better they like it, the better they like their jobs, and the better their general state of mind. However, these benefits may not be due solely to the increased earnings but also to factors associated with pay (prestige, security, etc.).

2. Workers who are more satisfied with their pay are more likely to like their jobs better, and are less likely to quit, be absent, or strike.

3. Job performance is not appreciably better on the part of workers who are higher paid or those who are better satisfied with their pay (unless pay is linked to performance, as in 6 below).

4. Workers who are underpaid, relative to those with whom they compare themselves, are likely to be dissatisfied with their pay.

5. Workers who are overpaid, relative to their contributions, tend also to be less satisfied; those on piece or incentive rates are prone to restrict output.

6. Pay plans (incentives, bonuses, etc.) which are linked to performance usually generate higher levels of work motivation and higher levels of performance or productivity.

7. However, this is unlikely to be true unless the workers understand the relationship between their performance and their pay, and unless they are confident that increased production will not result in changes in the pay rates or standards.

8. Where the work requires close cooperation, group incentive plans generate better results in terms of productivity than individual incentives; however, in general, group plans do not appear to improve productivity as much as individual plans, particularly when the groups are large.

9. Satisfaction with pay seems to be greater if it is tied to performance; under this circumstance, the correlation between performance and satisfaction with pay is also likely to be greater.

10. Pay-for-performance plans are not without their problems, particularly when there is job insecurity, when there are frequent changes in markets or methods, when not all important aspects of performance can be quantified, and when there is a climate of mistrust.

11. There is little firm evidence on the effects of other aspects of compensation systems, such as schedules of payment, secrecy, etc.

12. Some of the more recent issues in compensation policy include conversion of hourly to salaried basis, guaranteed annual wage, and payment on the basis of number of different tasks learned, but firm data as a guide to policy decisions are lacking.

There is substantial research evidence to support the contention that compensation linked to employee performance can have a very positive effect on productivity. While most of this research has not been geared specifically to the public sector, it is sufficiently broad to apply to government situations. Most local governments do not link compensation to employee performance except in very limited ways, and the eight cities participating in the project do not appear to be substantially different. Some of the cities have taken steps in this direction, though—most notably Dayton, Savannah, and Lakewood. However, there is now a vast array of information available that would permit cities to experiment with various plans of performance pay.

Employee Performance Appraisal

After pointing out the importance of rewarding and recognizing superior performance by employees and of ensuring that only those who perform actually receive the rewards available, it seems almost redundant to discuss the need to accurately evaluate employees' performance. How could one expect to reward superior performance without evaluating performance? The answer, of course, is that one cannot. Yet, as strange as it sounds, this is just what many, if not most, government officials in the cities attempt to do. The situation may not be as bad as what The Brookings Institution evaluators found in their important study of the city of New York personnel system in the early 1960s—far less than 1 percent of the performance ratings they reviewed indicated less than competent performance.[9] Nevertheless, in many city governments, almost everyone seems to be rated as acceptable or superior in the performance of their jobs.

There do not seem to be adequate incentives for supervisors to do a better job of evaluating their subordinates' performance. Managers and supervisors are abetted, perhaps encouraged, in their inadequate appraisals of employee performance. The reality is that in many organizations, if a supervisor rated half his subordinates as performing at unacceptable levels, then the organizational issue most likely to arise would concern the supervisor's capability to manage and direct the employees.

The basic inadequacy of employee performance appraisal in most cities is compounded by the severely limited number of techniques of evaluation that are actually used and by the misuse of those techniques or methods, principally the application of purpose-specific evaluation methods to multiple uses. For example, it is very common in city governments to have an established employee performance appraisal procedure that requires supervisors to complete a standard performance rating form for each employee every 6 or 12 months. It also is common for that to be the only formally recognized performance appraisal of those employees. However, the rating forms frequently then are used for such purposes as: (1) supervisors' suggestions to employees about aspects of their performance that need improvement, (2) determining whether employees receive periodic merit pay increases and promotions, (3) helping to rank employees for promotional consideration for more responsible positions, and (4) identifying employees' needs for specific types of training and developmental opportunities.

These and perhaps other distinct purposes of employee performance appraisal may require vastly different methods and approaches. For example, on the subject of improving employees' performance, there is now a considerable body of consistent research opinion that supervisory criticism of employees' performance is unlikely to lead to better performance and in fact may lead to worse performance. Far more likely to achieve results is the less threatening approach of mutual goal setting and review of progress. This type of approach, however, requires also that review of performance not be reserved for a formal performance review interview (although such interviews can be worthwhile when used appropriately) but instead be a continuous, day-to-day process.

The use of performance evaluations to predict success in another higher-level job is fraught with difficulty. There is not necessarily a very strong relationship between performance in one job and predictable performance in an entirely different job. This is especially true when the present job and the prospective job involve significant differences in job content, responsibility, and authority. The fact that someone "gets along well with fellow workers," for instance, is not likely to be of much value in predicting that person's capability to supervise others.

There has been a considerable amount of work done and research literature produced on measuring the outputs of governmental services and of the individuals who provide those services. Much of the available information is the result of the efforts of the Urban Institute, the International City Management Association, the National Commission on Productivity (and its successor, the National Center for Productivity and the Quality of Working Life), the National Science Foundation, and the Department of Housing and Urban Development (particularly the Policy Development and Research Division). This does not mean to slight the valuable contributions of other individuals and organizations, but these groups have been the most conspicuously involved.

To a large extent, the information needed for developing acceptable performance evaluation methods and plans for many of a city government's programs and workers already is available. Usable output measures have been put forward for many basic city services, especially for the direct-product services like solid waste collection, waste water treatment, and street maintenance, and even for some of the not so easily measured services like crime control, fire protection, and recreation services. There is also information available on citizen satisfaction measures for services that involve direct client relationships, such as health clinics. In some cases, there is need for consolidated measures, with indicators of the quality and quantity of directly measurable outputs and indicators of citizen satisfaction with the services provided. The point is that these types of performance measures, which in many cases have already been developed and tested, can be applied to the evaluation of individual employees' performance without a great deal of difficulty and cost.

There also are techniques available for evaluating the performance of government programs and employees who do not produce clearly definable and measurable "products" nor have direct client relations with the citizens.

This group includes many of the administrative employees of the government. One way of overcoming the measurement and evaluation problems related to these workers is the use of unit performance measures (for example, achievement of organizational unit objectives and, perhaps, indicators of user satisfaction) in tandem with peer review of the performance of individual employees.

The most important aspect of employee performance appraisal is the basis on which the employee is evaluated. Performance appraisal is of little value unless both the employee and the person(s) doing the evaluating have a clear understanding of, and have mutually agreed to, the basis of evaluation. Both must know in advance how the employee will be evaluated and why, and both must be fully convinced that the performance appraisal assesses real performance.

Employee Selection

One of the primary steps in the development of a productive workforce is, of course, the selection of highly qualified employees who can be expected to perform well. However, in the past few years, employee selection has become one of the most legalistic aspects of personnel management. It has generated multitudes of lawsuits, regulations, and general debate. The big event in employee selection since the initial adoption of merit hiring principles has been the impact of equal employment opportunity statutes and judicial decisions.

A short-run byproduct of the enormous attention to developing and validating reliable job and performance-related selection devices appears to be an increase in current skepticism that it is even possible to design completely objective predictors of the capabilities and probable job performance of new employees. One factor that has added fuel to this skepticism and caused frustration for responsible management officials in local governments has been the nearly absolute devotion of the U.S. Civil Service Commission and others to the "rule of three" and other similar selection restrictions.[10] At this juncture, managers in local governments generally have very little confidence in the ability of their standard tests and other selection devices to reliably make even basic distinctions between well-qualified, qualified, and unqualified applicants for government jobs. To them, making an arbitrary distinction between one group of candidates (whether one, three, five, or any other number of candidates) who scored above 95 percent on a standard test and other candidates who scored as high as 94.9 percent goes directly in the face of reason and undermines the concept of merit hiring.

Furthermore, local governments have received conflicting guidance and pressures from different sources in the federal and state governments. The agencies most concerned with equal employment opportunity are pushing affirmative action to hire more minorities and women. Those agencies most concerned with maintaining the integrity of the merit system are pushing for limited certification of eligible candidates for employment. Meanwhile, according to some local officials we have talked with, test psychologists and evaluators are telling local governments that their selection devices are incapable of reliably distinguishing between applicants whose eligibility ratings differ by as much as ten points.

There are dangers in unreasonable restrictions on selection practices that go beyond the simple frustration of local government managers. The major one is the possibility of discouraging good management and supervision of employees. Supervisors who have not had any significant role in selecting employees and who are convinced that the selection methods are unreasonable may feel that they have less stake in encouraging and assisting the performance of those employees than they would have if they had participated in (or at least felt confident in) the selection process. Most managers and supervisors with whom we have talked have expressed the firm conviction that they have little if any responsibility for deciding who is hired by the government when the "rule of three" and other restrictive rules are in operation, and they appear to be just as convinced that the supposedly objective selection process is unreasonable, probably is discriminatory, and undermines the selection of the best-qualified candidates for employment.

Employee Development

The big question on employee development and training is: If it is such a good thing, why do governments do so little of it? Governments are being pressed to do more and different things, to provide sometimes different and always better services, to do what they do in different and better ways, to get greater productivity from every government worker—all of which means *change*. Costs change, revenues change, the characteristics of the population change, service needs change, the whole job of government changes. Government's workers must change, too. They must refine their skills, obtain new skills, develop new abilities, in some cases learn specialized techniques and skills, and in other cases broaden their specialized skills into more general abilities. Governments must develop the capability to manage under changing circumstances.

One of the most important tasks in personnel management is ensuring that government workers—from the top all the way down through the organization—have the knowledge and skills they need to perform their jobs at the top of their capabilities. How well this management task is carried out in a government can have a significant effect on the performance of individual employees and on the overall productivity of the government. What is sometimes confounding is that while there is widespread recognition of the importance of employee development and training, the amount of resources that governments generally devote to training is very small. The eight-city survey provided one demonstration of the perceived significance of employee development: more than 60 percent of the survey respondents felt that employee-development factors had helped their cities' productivity efforts. Yet more than 70 percent of the respondents, on average, felt that each of the listed employee-development factors could have provided greater support to productivity actions.

Data reported by the International City Management Association (ICMA), based on a survey of city governments, reflect the low level of funding for training.[11] More than 75 percent of all the cities responding spent less than $25,000 on training, and over half of them spent less than $10,000 (in the fiscal year that included January 1, 1974). Of the cities with populations of 100,000 or greater, approximately three-fourths devoted less than $\frac{1}{10}$ of 1 percent of their operating budgets to training.

The main reason for the low funding priority for training appears to be the lack of clearly demonstrable direct results. In a situation where the local government may be cutting back services, perhaps having to increase taxes, and where large numbers of skilled workers are unemployed, it can be politically difficult to justify spending scarce public monies to provide needed training for public employees. Furthermore, in many communities, government workers on the whole have fairly high incomes relative to the general population. It is easy to conceive of complaints that at the salaries the government pays, it should be able to get qualified people and not have to train them. This means that devoting resources to training and development of the workforce may require greater justification than many other kinds of government expenditures, but it does not mean that training resources are not justifiable. On the contrary, they can be justified on the basis of evaluations of the benefits of the training.

Local governments seem to have particular difficulty in justifying, either to themselves or to the public, the expenditure of funds for management training or training for middle- and upper-level administrative personnel. The elected and appointed policy officials of the governments frequently express their support and commitment for training and development, but in the budget-making process their commitment seems to wane. There are other, more pressing needs, there is no hard evidence that the training will produce the desired results, the people who would be trained are too critical to the government to lose time from the jobs while in training—these are some of the customary reasons for the failure to support training.

Other More Pressing Needs. This observation may be more apparent than real. Increased training, if properly designed and conducted, can lead to both greater efficiency and effectiveness in achieving the government's aims. If people do their jobs better, more quickly, and at lower costs, then the government will be in even better position to meet the "pressing needs."

Potential Trainees Are Too Critical. The fact that individuals are critical to the organization may be the best reason for having them trained. Both this argument and the previous one really are based on questioning the results of training; that is, the decision makers are not convinced that the training will produce benefits that will be greater than would be produced if the funds were spent on other needs or than would be produced simply by having the proposed trainees on the job.

Lack of Evidence on Results. Most local governments in fact have not sought the evidence that would demonstrate the results of training. The ICMA year-book notes: "Many cities make no attempt to evaluate their training programs and in cities that do conduct evaluations there is little evidence to suggest that evaluations are part of an ongoing attempt to compare training goals and objectives [with results]."[12] The usual reason for the lack of evaluations of training is that evaluation is expensive and difficult.

As more and more local governments establish performance measurement systems, however, there is less need to start from scratch in designing measures for evaluating training. The most basic measure of training success is change in employee and organizational performance. Local government officials should recognize this and should proceed to establish mechanisms for evaluating the cost-effectiveness of existing training programs and analyzing the cost and effectiveness of proposed training. Such mechanisms will help to ensure that the purposes of training are more carefully and clearly defined, that the training is designed to meet these purposes, and that the results can be evaluated against these purposes.

Another observation about training and employee development in the cities came from the eight-city survey results. When asked which of the employee-development factors could have provided the greatest support of their citys' productivity actions, the largest number of respondents chose "procedures for matching training to the actual needs of employees." In order to have a positive effect on the performance of the organization and of individual employees in the organization, it is necessary to have effective means of identifying the needs of employees for training and to ensure that the training that is offered actually meets those needs. Otherwise, there is no way that the government can expect training to have its desired results. Not surprisingly, the organizational and employee performance measures that have been discussed many times in this book can provide very useful information on the training needs of employees.

Collective Bargaining

Collective bargaining, or labor-management relations, has become one of the central issues in any discussion of public management. Chester Newland has called it the "greatest personnel 'add-on' of all times" and described it as a "development since the 1950s that threatens or promises (depending on one's viewpoint) to reverse which function is the add-on and then to become the central thrust of public personnel administration."[13] One of the major debates in public management circles in recent years has focused on whether collective bargaining and merit principles of employment are in significant conflict with one another.[14] In one of the more recent articles on the subject, an official of the U.S. Civil Service Commission, who has long been involved in the administration and enforcement of the federal "Standards for a Merit System of Personnel Administration," presented his thoughts on how a successful "marriage" of collective bargaining and merit systems can be forged.[15]

The number and percentage of local government workers who are unionized has grown tremendously in recent years, and many commentators expect the growth to continue, although probably at a slower rate. Others see a leveling off in unionization of government employees. In either case, collective bargaining can be expected to grow, whether quantitatively or qualitatively. In many cities where portions of the workforce are unionized, the scope of bargaining is still very limited, focusing almost exclusively on base pay rates for union members. The trend, however, appears to be toward expanding the scope of bargaining to such areas as hours and working conditions, layoff rules, promotion rules, new-hire selection rules, job titles and classifications, employee grievance machinery and procedures, impasse-resolution procedures, and other important issues concerning the workforce. It is clear that in many cities collective bargaining already has a significant impact on governmental performance and productivity, that it is likely to continue having an impact in those cities, and that it probably will have important effects in the cities that have yet to feel its impact.

It is clear, also, that while the effects of collective bargaining are potentially advantageous for productivity, there also is the potential for disadvantageous effects. Several aspects of collective bargaining are particularly important. One of these is the question of the number and size of separate units of employees for bargaining purposes. The usual criterion for determining bargaining units is a definable "community of interest" among employees to be included in a unit. In practice, the community of interest has been described in various ways—some governments have apparently found a community of interest only among the employees in a particular job class and have, accordingly, established each job title as a separate bargaining unit; others have set entire departments as bargaining units, even including upper-level supervisors and managers.[16] Either situation causes problems. Large numbers of small bargaining units mean extra time and costs for the government in negotiating separately with them and in coordinating the numerous separate contracts. There also is the danger of competition between the different units in terms of what concessions they obtain from the management negotiators. Overly broad bargaining units can lead to unjustified across-the-board wage settlements and also may raise the question, "If managers are in the same unions as their employees, who's minding the store—who sits on the management side of the bargaining table?"

Another area that has caused difficulty and controversy recently is that of binding arbitration. It is not so much the concept that gives rise to the problems, but rather the results that have been seen to occur. There are fundamental differences between private industrial labor relations and collective bargaining in government, just as there are differences in the missions of private and public organizations. Largely because of the fairly short history of collective bargaining in the public sector, there may be a shortage of capable arbitrators who recognize and understand these differences. Some local governments have become dissatisfied with the practice of binding arbitration for settling negotiation or grievance impasses. They have found that the recognized arbitrators hand down decisions that might be workable in private industry but that, they feel, are completely unworkable in a government organization providing critical services to the public.

An additional issue that has caused disagreement between unions and management in many local governments is that of performance measurement. Especially troubling to union representatives in many cases is the use of performance measures at the individual employee level. Generally, the unions argue that the performance-evaluation techniques and measures that are in use or proposed for use are neither objective nor accurate indicators of employees' performance.[17] Additionally, union representatives may have a predictable bias against individual employee performance measures because they might tend to work to the disadvantage of at least some of the union members in the government workforce. The unions generally appear to favor organizational and unit performance measures; and if pay is tied to performance, they prefer across-the-board pay changes based on organizational performance. However, group pay incentives for performance are unlikely to have much impact unless the group is truly a team engaged in work that requires a closely coordinated team effort. Incentive pay tied to individual employee performance, when coupled with acceptable and accurate performance measures, is much more likely to have a positive impact on worker motivation and productivity.

A similar kind of debate centers on the question of rules governing major personnel management decisions like promotions and reductions in force. Government employee unions traditionally have pushed hard for seniority as the principal basis for promotional consideration and also for determining how reductions in force or layoffs should be handled ("last hired, first fired"). Again, union representatives frequently assert that most measures for predicting future job performance (for example, promotion tests) and of evaluating previous performance are not sufficiently accurate and valid. They claim that seniority is a better indicator, at least for the initial decision as to who should be considered for promotional opportunities. Similar arguments are made on determining who gets laid off in reductions in force.

A final aspect of collective bargaining that has been the subject of much discussion in local governments is that of "productivity bargaining." For the most part, productivity bargaining in cities has been of two kinds: (1) so-called buyout bargaining, in which management's aim has been to do away with or change existing contract provisions relating to work practices or compensation which impede the effectiveness or efficiency of operations, and (2) gain-sharing, in which management agrees to share with workers the cost savings resulting from increased organizational output. More recently, an additional kind of productivity bargaining has occurred in some instances, and we call it "rock-bottom bargaining." Some cities, most notably New York City, have reached the point where they are no longer able to compensate workers for cutting out expensive contract provisions (buyout) or to share direct cost savings with the workers. Their financial condition is such that reducing costs is the only alternative to laying off workers.[18] In these cases, the bargaining issues focus on ways that management and labor can agree to cut costs without reducing the labor force, or to reduce the size of the layoffs that otherwise would be necessary.

Some cases of productivity bargaining have had results that could hardly be called productivity improvements; productivity provisions in some collective bargaining agreements have not been renewed because of either management or union dissatisfaction with their implementation; and in some cases attempts at productivity bargaining have led to the worsening of relations between management and workers.[19] More promising than the somewhat limited concept of productivity bargaining are the cooperative labor-management committees that have been established in a number of cities and other units of government.[20] In the long run, what is really needed is a continuing dialogue between management representatives of the government and representatives of the employee unions to deal with many of the extremely complex issues of the workforce and its performance.

Employee-Employer Relations and Supervision

In developing the instrument for use in the eight-city survey, we purposefully included a section on employee-employer relations. The factors listed in that section of the survey instrument were described specifically in terms of consultation with or involvement of employees in the development and implementation of cities' productivity actions. An important indication of an organization's effectiveness is its ability to deal with external change and to continually change itself. In effect, change is what productivity improvement is about—making the right changes for the organization and its subunits (down to the individual employee unit) to be more effective and efficient. The section on employee-employer relations was intended to ascertain whether the respondents viewed employee involvement in the change process as important to improving productivity, what kind of effect employee participation had had, and whether greater employee-employer consultation was needed.

The survey results bore out what other research has established, which basically is that the chances of success in trying to improve government productivity will be greatly enhanced if employees are consulted early and participate as much as possible in the planning, design, and implementation of the changes undertaken. Furthermore, while majorities of the respondents perceived each of the employee-employer relations factors that were listed as having helped their cities' productivity actions, even more substantial majorities saw the potential for greater support, presumably through more involvement of employees in decisions related to productivity improvement.

The employee-employer relations factors listed in the survey instrument all dealt with aspects of employee involvement in the "planning, development, and implementation of productivity actions." The results of the survey, while they deal explicitly with some of the cities' specific efforts to improve productivity, could apply to almost any program, policy, or structural change in the government organization. Front-line employees frequently are able to provide valuable insights into the likely consequences of proposed changes—consequences that might otherwise be overlooked. In addition, they may be able to contribute knowledgeably to assessing the potential effectiveness and costs of various program and policy alternatives. Most important, however, the employees are the ones who have to carry out the changes. If they have participated fully in the planning and development of the changes, they will have helped to ensure the reasonableness of the changes and simultaneously may have developed a sense of "ownership" of the new policies and programs, a greater sense of commitment to their success. Employee participation can help to defuse the threat that is invariably seen in "management-engineered" changes.

This discussion of employee-employer relations leads logically into the broader questions of supervision and direction of employees. Supervision was not included as a specific component of personnel management in the eight-city survey. It is a dimension of management that cuts across the various components and is more attitudinal than it is systems oriented. Yet the quality of supervision in an organization overall may have far more to do with that organization's performance and productivity than do the separate components of personnel management. However, quality supervision in a large organization is impossible without those components and the effective functioning of the "systems" they imply. For example, an important part of supervision is the accurate evaluation of subordinate employees' performance, but this aspect of supervision may be limited by the characteristics of the existing performance-appraisal system.

Effective supervision requires the fulfillment of a variety of interrelated roles that are hard to define or assess in measurable terms—either quality or quantity measures. Effective supervision requires that managers and supervisors ensure that:

Employees, both individually and collectively, have a clear understanding and appreciation of how they "fit" in the overall organization

Employees understand fully what is expected of them and why—what they are expected to produce and how it contributes to achieving the government's missions

Employees have the necessary information and support, skills and abilities, and responsibility and flexibility to produce what is expected of them

All employees are dealt with fairly and equitably

Employees know how well they are performing, or how they are perceived to be performing

Performance is always encouraged, superior performance is recognized, and the superior performer is rewarded.

These are the basic roles that supervision must fill, but it is doubtful that they are in fact being filled adequately in most city governments. Because supervision is such a broad and amorphous subject, there has been little hard research on the links between it and productivity. However, there has been some research on the question of how supervision affects workers' job satisfaction. An example is the survey of over 4,000 state and local government employees conducted by the National Training and Development Service (NTDS). NTDS has reported that its survey found "supervisory relations to be the biggest source of friction for public employees."[21] While it may be difficult, as we indicated earlier, to measure the effectiveness of supervision, the NTDS project points up one method of gaining some indication of performance—the employee survey.

Actually, any government seeking to influence productivity through better supervision should develop reasonable measures of supervisory performance that can be repeated periodically. These measures likely would include the integration of several different performance indicators, such as:

Organizational unit performance indicators:

Direct output indicators

Client or user satisfaction indicators

Supervisory evaluations (e.g., department head's evaluations of the supervisors in the department)

Subordinate appraisals (e.g., evaluation of supervisors by their subordinates)

Quality of supervision "symptoms" (e.g., leave usage, employee grievances or complaints, etc., within each supervisor's unit).

A great deal of information is gathered in a city government which, if combined sensibly, can provide significant indications of the effectiveness of supervision in the government overall and in its organizational units.

The combined information may not constitute "measures of effectiveness" in the sense that we normally would use that term, but it should be very useful for purposes of improving supervision in the government.

Conclusion

In summary, there are a number of critical aspects of personnel management in city governments that have a very substantial impact on the governments' overall performance and productivity. Without doubt, many of the traditional systems, practices, and procedures that have grown up around the concept of merit employment pose significant barriers to improving the productivity of governments. They especially do not provide adequate incentives to managers to manage well or to employees to perform well—in short, performance does not appear to be the central theme of many established systems of personnel management. This does not mean that the concepts or principles of merit employment in government should be challenged. On the contrary, it is meant to challenge the shrouding of incompetence, inflexibility, invalidity, inaccuracy, and unreasonableness in the cloak of merit. Merit is what is needed; it frequently is not what exists. In effect, in terms of hiring, merit should mean, the capability to perform and the likelihood of good performance; and in other personnel management decisions, it should mean job performance as the basis of personnel actions taken.

Various alternatives have been proposed to the traditional civil service commission form of personnel structure for governments. Most of them have as a central aim the clear establishment of "accountability" for personnel management in the hands of those who are held accountable for managing the government. We did not set out to evaluate alternatives to traditional personnel systems, although we believe the results of the project as contained in this book will be useful to others in assessing alternatives. However, a couple of comments about alternatives are in order. The results of the eight-city survey and of other relevant research that we have reviewed indicate to us that the establishment of greater authority and accountability for personnel management in the cities is needed. Along with the authority would go the flexibility to get the job done, that is, without unnecessary restrictions and regulations that generally add nothing but complications and a veneer of legalism to the processes. At the same time, one of the aims that is inherent in the civil service commission type of system must be preserved. It concerns the protection of employees from unjustified coercion and adverse action by management. Particularly, provision must be maintained for protecting "whistle-blowers" in the government. If an employee knows that his superior grossly mismanages the public's funds or misuses the public trust for personal financial gain, we would want this employee to "blow the whistle," not stay quiet because his job depends on his silence.

The greatest change in personnel management in the cities that our research indicates is the building-in of productivity or performance measurement and evaluation as the critical ingredients in all the processes and decisions. As we have indicated, the capability of adequately measuring performance in many governmental functions and of many city workers already exists. To achieve greater productivity in the government through better personnel management clearly requires the use of performance measurement as the basis for personnel-related decisions.

Notes

1. Raymond A. Katzell et al. *Work, Productivity, and Job Satisfaction: An Evaluation of Policy Related Research* (New York: The Psychological Corporation, January 1975), p. 25. Reproduced by permission. Copyright © 1975 by New York University. Published by The Psychological Corporation. All rights reserved.

2. Ibid., p. 24.

3. Ibid., pp. 38-39.

4. Ibid., p. 24.

5. U.S. Civil Service Commission, *Job Analysis, Developing and Documenting Data*, BIPP 152-63 (Washington, D.C.: U.S. Civil Service Commission, Bureau of Intergovernmental Personnel Programs, November 1975).

6. F. Herzberg, B. Mausner, and B. Snyderman, *The Motivation to Work* (New York: Wiley, 1959).

7. Abraham H. Maslow, *Motivation and Personality* (New York: Harper and Brothers, 1954).

8. Katzell et al., pp. 332-334.

9. David T. Stanley, *Professional Personnel for the City of New York* (Washington, D.C.: The Brookings Institution, 1963).

10. Proposed "Uniform Guidelines on Employee Selection Procedures" were published in December 1977 by the Civil Service Commission, Equal Employment Opportunity Commission, Department of Justice, and Department of Labor. They would replace the existing federal executive agency guidelines and the EEOC's separate guidelines. The proposed new guidelines would represent both a uniform federal stance on employee selection requirements and a more flexible approach to meeting selection principles. Upon taking effect, the "Uniform Guidelines" would supersede the existing requirements of the federal agencies with respect to selection, including the selection portion of CSC's Standards for a Merit System of Personnel Administration.

11. The International City Management Association, *The Municipal Yearbook 1976* (Washington, D.C., 1976), p. 188.

12. Ibid., p. 185.

13. Chester A. Newland, "Public Personnel Administration: Legalistic Reforms vs. Effectiveness, Efficiency, and Economy," *Public Administration Review* 36(5): 532, September-October 1976.

14. See Stanley D. Nollen, *The Effect of Collective Bargaining on Municipal Personnel Systems: A Research Review* (Washington, D.C.: Public Services Laboratory, Georgetown University, 1975).

15. Douglas I. McIntyre, "Merit Principles and Collective Bargaining: A Marriage or Divorce," *Public Administration Review* 37(2): 186-190, March-April 1977.

16. R.T. Jones, *Public Sector Labor Relations: An Evaluation of Policy Related Research* (Belmont, Mass.: Contract Research Corporation, February 1975).

17. Nollen, *The Effect of Collective Bargaining*.

18. K. Auletta, "More for Less," *The New Yorker*, August 1, 1977, pp. 30-48.

19. Raymond D. Horton, "Productivity and Productivity Bargaining in Government: A Critical Analysis," *Public Administration Review* 36(4): 407-414, July-August 1976.

20. The National Center for Productivity and Quality of Working Life issued a request for proposals in August 1977 for conducting research on and writing case histories of a network of state and local government labor-management committees. The products should provide useful additional information about such committees.

21. Katherine C. Janka et al., *People Performance. . .Results* (Washington, D.C.: National Training and Development Service Press, 1977), p. 32.

6 An Outline of Future Research

In this chapter, a partial agenda for further research is set forth. The agenda is not intended to document the many gaps that exist in research on personnel management an' productivity. Rather, the agenda draws on the findings of the work already completed during the first phase of the current study plan to identify what appears to be a major question requiring further study. City officials who collaborated in the study have identified a number of research issues that are of particular significance now to their own cities and, very likely, to many others. Among them are the following:

1. Can a system be developed to provide incentives and rewards for managerial performance, to improve the quality of management in the city?
2. How can the city's compensation system be improved to better meet the city's needs and objectives, including greater productivity?
3. What alternatives to traditional forms of compensation can be used to motivate employees to higher productivity?
4. What measurable relationships can be determined between incentiv ; and performance criteria?
5. Can both the qualitative and quantitative values of different levels of employee performance be reliably determined?
6. What types of mechanisms can be used to bind employee-performance-incentive agreements?
7. Is there a need to have a city civil service commission, given the current and expanding scope of collective bargaining?
8. How does the city's existing "promotion from within" rule affect the development of an effective managerial workforce?
9. What steps can be taken to improve Affirmative Action in filling management positions, while simultaneously improving productivity?
10. How can the city best ensure effective union participation in productivity-improvement efforts?
11. Should such currently separate activities as labor-management relations and employee training be integrated into a comprehensive personnel management program?

Discussion of these diverse yet intertwined questions brought about agreement that the central theme of most of them was the application of productivity or performance criteria in personnel management. One potential issue for consideration was why cities generally have not applied productivity measurement widely, particularly for personnel management purposes. The broader, especially significant research issue is the overall process of making changes in management techniques and methods in city governments, of which the application of productivity measurement in personnel management is a very important late step.

The Core Policy Issues

In the past several years, repeated emphasis has been given to the importance of building management capacity and enhancing productivity in the cities. The extent of federal grant assistance to the cities and the increasing dependency of the cities on grants in aid underlie these efforts. The National Center for Productivity and the Quality of Working Life (and its predecessor, the National Commission on Productivity), despite limited funding, has provided considerable encouragement for the measurement and improvement of productivity, but the gap between developing measures and applying them remains wide. The National Science Foundation has funded numerous individual projects and programs related to productivity. NSF also has sponsored several consortia of cities—large, medium-sized, and relatively small—to encourage, by collaborative undertakings in a number of cities, the introduction of new technology, better understanding of management capacity requirements, and the application of scientific advances to city government. The Department of Housing and Urban Development also has been substantively involved in financing the development or demonstration of productivity measurements and other management processes for cities, as has the U.S. Civil Service Commission (IPA program), in a more limited way. At present, an effort is underway under the auspices of the President's Office of Science and Technology Policy to define major problems in states and cities that pose questions for scientific exploration and that could by their solution enhance productivity.

Three core policy issues emerge from the work that has been done and the results that have been achieved. The first is primarily of relevance to federal decision makers. The second and third, however, have considerable relevance for both local government policymakers and those in the federal and state governments who have an interest in local management capabilities.

1. *Should the federal government provide substantial assistance to cities to encourage the buildup of management capacity?* The joint OMB/NSF-sponsored Study Committee on Policy Management Assistance (1975)[1] recommended more federal assistance for building central management capability, pointing to the imbalance between resources for program-by-program management efforts and for central administrative efforts. However, the tentative

recommendations of a recent General Accounting Office study on productivity suggest that a large general grant program would not efficiently achieve the purposes sought, largely because of the differences in the readiness of cities to adopt management changes.

2. *What elements or processes are essential to the buildup of management capacity and the achievement of enhanced productivity?* There is growing recognition of the importance of personnel or human resources management in achieving greater productivity. But there is little understanding of the elements or processes that lead to the application of performance measures in managing government personnel for improved productivity.

3. *Has the past expenditure of federal resources (funds and technical assistance) on productivity measurement and management improvement produced the appropriate results in personnel management?* Substantial effort has gone into developing and demonstrating productivity measures, technology-transfer processes, and other management improvements. Yet there is a wide gap between development and application. Part of the gap may be explained by a natural diffusion lag. A significant part of the gap also may be due to the differences among cities in their readiness to adopt changes or new techniques. If the expected result of the federal effort was wide-spread application of the management innovations that have been developed, it may be that such a result will be achieved over a longer period of time, as more cities reach readiness.

Productivity improvement in the cities is dependent upon productive and effective public servants. While the performance of government workers determines productivity, it is conditioned by the governments' personnel management policies, procedures, and practices. One concept that was clearly and repeatedly suggested by our work is the need for applying productivity-performance measures in personnel management programs and decisions.

What Is the Hypothesis?

The primary hypothesis is that the development and implementation of productivity criteria in personnel management are late-stage applications of analytical effort and productivity measurement. Formulating the hypothesis in this way is not intended to suggest that personnel management represents a lower-order application of productivity measurements. On the contrary, the hypothesis carries with it the implication that a substantial period of analysis and productivity measurement is needed before the measurements can be incorporated into the system of personnel management, for example, in employee compensation and promotion. These applications require much previous experimentation and the use of productivity measurement in a variety of management circumstances so that they have become familiar.

Why studying this hypothesis is important perhaps requires more elaboration. There is much concern about relating promotion and compensation to individual employee performance, as measured by productivity criteria, as a reward or incentive system. This application makes operational at a very specific level the work on productivity and analysis that has been going on for the past decade or so. Which cities are likely to move in the direction of applying productivity measurement to personnel management? Which cities would face major difficulties in attempting such moves? If we could establish something about the past experience with processes, we would have a better basis for predicting success or failure. We also would have a better basis for guiding federal policies on aids for management capacity building. As important, if not more so, such information would be of very great value to city government policy makers in helping them recognize the important steps that may need to be taken—the processes and capabilities developed—if they are to be able to successfully apply productivity measurement in personnel management.

What are the operational conditions that accommodate management innovation and facilitate application of productivity measures in personnel management? An understanding of the determinants would illuminate the question by clarifying the characteristics of the cities and staffs that either accelerate the process of analysis and measurement application in management or impede that process.

Management innovation appears to be a cumulative process, in which each management change (and the additional experience that accompanies it) is the building block of subsequent changes. For example, there was considerable encouragement and some financial support for cities in the 1960s to implement planning-programming-budgeting systems (PPBS) along the lines of a federal model. Many, if not most, of the efforts undertaken in local governments were less than completely successful. In hindsight, it appears that one of the primary reasons for the lack of success was that the cities did not have an existing policy-analysis staff capability prior to going into PPBS, and policy-analysis capability was the linchpin of PPBS. However, the PPBS experience in many cities may not have been a complete failure, because through that effort they developed such an analytic capacity, which became the building block of subsequent changes in management methods like Management by Objectives, program evaluation, and Zero-Base Budgeting.

The Model

In order to test the hypothesis, a simple model is posited. The development and application of productivity measurements in a city government are assumed to be a function of five sets of characteristics: demographic-economic, fiscal, structural, innovative-incentive, and technological. Symbolically, this can be written as follows:

$$P = f(D, F, S, I, T)$$

where P = the process of developing and applying productivity measurements

D = a set of demographic-economic characteristics of the jurisdiction (e.g., population size, per capita income, unemployment rate, geographic location)

F = a set of fiscal characteristics (e.g., per capita general expenditures, changes in tax effort)

S = a set of structural characteristics of the government (e.g., form of government, management salary structure, extent of local appropriations for management changes or productivity measurement)

I = a set of organizational and attitudinal characteristics that act as incentives to innovation (e.g., availability of slack resources, extent of management training, willingness to attempt risky innovations)

T = a set of technology characteristics (e.g., the number of research or technology-related projects funded by the federal government, the number of interjurisdictional technology projects the city has participated in)

The following hypothesized relationships, among others, warrant examination through an empirical test of the model:

Larger cities are more likely to apply productivity measurements and to have introduced work on outcome measurement earlier than smaller cities.

The higher the income of the residents of the city, the more likely the pressures for accountability and measurement.

The higher the rate of unemployment, the greater the fiscal stress and need to achieve greater productivity.

The higher per capita expenditures, the more likely productivity assessment.

The larger the increases in tax efforts, the more likely productivity assessment.

Federal project grants have encouraged and financed a number of the city steps taken toward analysis and productivity measurement.

Cities with higher management salaries are more innovative and more likely to have introduced systems of measurement.

Manager cities have launched measurement systems and applied such measures more often and earlier than nonmanager cities, and have taken on management-improvement projects that call for collaborative work among cities more often.

Productivity assessment and technology transfer are closely related, and the larger the numbers of technology-transfer projects launched, the more likely productivity assessment and application.

Recognition by elected officials of the importance of productivity assessment, as evidenced by separate appropriations, contributes importantly to productivity measurement and application.

Prior Research

The issue in question here has not been dealt with substantively in previous research. However, prior research dealing with innovation and the diffusion of innovations is highly pertinent. This research, according to Greer, can be classified into three approaches: the classical approach, the organizational approach, and the political approach.[2] Those who approach the subject from a classical point of view (Merton; Rogers; Rogers and Shoemaker; and Becker) examine the traits of the person who induces the application of a new idea.[3] Merton drew a dichotomy between "localites" and "cosmopolites." The former were content to function in the local community, while the latter derived satisfaction from participation in a number of communities with a national or global perspective (that is, professional organizations, national or international corporations). Cosmopolites are potential "opinion leaders" and the first to acquire information about available innovation.

Rogers and Rogers and Shoemaker developed the aspect of diffusion theory that examined the process of communicating a new idea to another person who subsequently adopts the idea. Becker found cosmopolites were people who usually chose low-risk innovations that had a high-adoption potential (HAP). Innovators who implemented ideas with low-adoption potential (LAP) were generally localite, older, not frequently innovative, but willing to take a high risk with one particular innovation.

While the classical approach emphasizes the individual's role in the innovation process, a second approach considers the influence of organizational structure (Bingham; Aiken and Hage; Meyer and Williams; Feller, Menzel, and Kozak; Roessner; Walker; Gray; Mansfield; and Zaltman, Duncan, and Holbeck).[4] This approach relies on the works of management theorists for its conceptual underpinnings. Bingham found that two organizational variables (unit size and resource availability) were significant in the adoption of innovations by local government units. This was valid, however, only for process innovations, those largely invisible to the general public. Organizational determinants of the more visible product innovations were less significant, suggesting perhaps that political factors need to be examined.

Walker and Gray considered innovation at the state level and found that organizations look toward opinion-leader organizations, causing diffusion to flow from the national level, to regional pioneers, to followers in parochial outposts. Walker identified innovation-determining factors, such as regionalism and the growing professionalism of public managers, and Gray documented patterns of diffusion that were particular to the type of innovation.

The third approach, which so far is less developed than the classical and organizational approaches, is the political approach (Dahl; Downs and Mohr; and Mohr).[5] Since successful innovation may result in unwanted change for certain vested interest groups, it is important to study how political resources are used to persuade or coerce groups to cooperate in the pursuit of goals desired by the innovating organization or leader. Dahl identified a number of political resources, including control over job, information or expertise, access to money or wealth, and esteem or social standing.

A study by Mohr, which contains elements of all three approaches, postulated that successful innovation will be positively related to the availability of resources and negatively related to political obstacles. He found that community size, financial resources, and the availability of trained supervisory personnel were highly correlated with successful innovation.

The General Outline of a Research Design

Much of the research just cited was of a case-study nature. The thrust of the research we are suggesting is the combination of the case-study method with a more aggregative approach. Two procedures to be undertaken simultaneously are recommended. The first is a case-by-case examination of experience in several medium-sized cities. The second involves a survey of approximately 600 randomly selected cities.

Study in selected cities would provide a set of cases that would be the basis for answering questions about what works to gain productivity applications in personnel management and, also, what combinations of circumstances lead to favorable action on new processes of management that incorporate productivity measurements. Each of the cities in our study was selected initially for its prior commitment to productivity improvement. It is to be expected that they and other innovative cities will take further actions in the period ahead toward improved personnel management. The types of actions that are proposed and the reception of those proposals politically in the cities would provide important inputs to the case materials. Where little in the way of changes in personnel management is proposed to improve productivity in the cities, the circumstances surrounding the inaction also would be addressed.

Representatives of the selected cities also could collaborate in the design of a survey instrument to be applied in surveying a stratified sample of approximately 600 U.S. cities. As responses to that survey are analyzed, the selected cities would give an indepth perspective to significant questions that are uncovered. Furthermore, through joint discussions of common problems and issues (a well-recognized benefit of the earlier collaboration), these cities would constitute an important review group, to identify questions about personnel management processes that require assessment and lend their experiences to other cities.

By simultaneously conducting a detailed examination of a few cities and a general examination of a large number of cities, the major hypothesis of the study—that the development and implementation of personnel performance criteria are late-stage applications of analytical, effort and productivity measurement—can be tested at both a micro and a macro level. Important questions about processes and productivity applications uncovered at the macro level can be further explored and perhaps explained with information developed at the micro level.

Notes

1. *Strengthening Public Management in the Intergovernmental System,* a report prepared for the Office of Management and Budget by the Study Committee on Policy Management Assistance, Executive Office of the President, Washington, D.C., 1975.

2. A.L. Greer, "Advances in the Study of Diffusion of Innovation in Health Care Organizations,"*Milbank Memorial Fund Quarterly* (forthcoming). Although this study focuses on innovation in the health care area, it provides a comprehensive review and bibliography of recent innovation literature. The literature discussion in our chapter is intended only as a summary of selected works.

3. R.K. Merton, *Social Theory and Social Structure* (New York: Free Press, 1949); E.M. Rogers, *Diffusion of Innovations* (New York: Free Press, 1972); E.M. Rogers, F.F. Shoemaker, *Communication of Innovations: A Cross Cultural Approach* (New York: Free Press, 1971); H.M. Becker, "Sociometric Location and Innovativeness: Reformulation and Extension of the Diffusion Model," *American Sociological Review* 35:267-282, 1970.

4. R.D. Bingham, *Innovation, Bureaucracy, and Public Policy: A Study of Innovation Adoption by Local Government* (Milwaukee, Wisconsin: Univ. of Wisconsin, Milwaukee, Urban Research Center, 1976); M. Aiken and J. Hage, "The Organic Organization and Innovation," *Sociology* 5:63-82, 1971; M. Meyer and W. Williams, "Comparison of Innovation in Public and Private Sectors. An Exploratory Study," University of California-Riverside, Report to NSF, 1976; I. Feller, D. Menzel, and L. Kozak, "The Diffusion of Innovation in Municipal Governments," final report to NSF; J.D. Roessner, "Federal Policy and the Application of Technology to State and Local Government Problems, *Policy Analysis* (forthcoming); J.L. Walker, "The Diffusion of

Innovation Among the American States," *American Political Science Review* 63:880-889, 1969; J.L. Walker, "Comment: Problems in Research on the Diffusion of Policy Innovations," *American Political Science Review* 67:1186-1191, 1973; V. Gray, "Innovation in the States: A Diffusion Study," *American Political Science Review* 67:1171-1185, 1973; E. Mansfield, "Speed of Response of Firms in New Techniques," *Quarterly Journal of Economics* 77:290-311, 1973; G. Zaltman, R. Duncan, and J. Holbeck, *Innovation and Organizations* (New York: Wiley, 1973).

5. R. Dahl, *Who Governs?* (New Haven: Yale Univ. Press, 1961); G.W. Downs, and L.B. Mohr, "Conceptual Issues in the Study of Innovation," paper delivered at the annual meeting of the American Political Science Association, San Francisco, 1975; L.B. Mohr, "Determinants of Innovation in Organizations," *American Political Science Review* 63:111-126, 1969.

Appendixes

Appendix A
Survey Administration
and the
Survey Instrument

In order to assess the interaction between personnel management and productivity improvement in eight cities, a survey instrument was developed and administered to 200 managerial employees. This appendix reports the details of survey administration and ends with the version of the survey used in one of the eight cities (Dayton, Ohio).

Overview of the Instrument

The general format of the survey questionnaire is to ask respondents four questions, each of which has multiple parts, about the interaction between personnel management and productivity improvement. After an introductory group of questions on the productivity actions, these four questions were then repeated ten times, each time about the interaction between a different component of personnel management and productivity improvement. The first of the four questions asked the respondent to indicate whether the particular component of personnel management (recruitment and selection, classification, compensation, performance appraisal, employee development, promotions/transfers/terminations, employee-employer relations, collective bargaining, Affirmative Action, and personnel staffing level decisions) had impeded, had no impact, or had helped the implementation of five to seven specific productivity actions in his or her city.

The second question in each section required the respondent to use his or her judgment in aggregating the individual productivity actions mentioned in the first section into a composite "productivity actions" and assess the direction of the impact of various factors within each of the components of personnel management on productivity actions in aggregate. The factors within each component of the personnel management function were selected to be the narrowest specification of the necessary activities within a particular component of a personnel function which we could reasonably expect line department managers to recognize easily. They capture the most important parts of each personnel component and are described in language which was not city-specific jargon. For each of the ten components of personnel management, the list of five to seven specific productivity actions undertaken in that city was repeated in the question directly above this one to keep an operational definition of productivity actions fresh in the minds of the respondents.

The third question pursued issues raised in the second question by asking which of the factors within that component of personnel management *could* have provided greater support to the implementation of the city productivity actions. If more than one factor was indicated, the respondents were also asked to indicate which of the factors could have provided the greatest support.

Finally, a fourth question (labeled Section B within each component of personnel management) asked about the impact of productivity actions on the effectiveness and the cost of the ten components of personnel management.

For further details on the survey instrument, the reader is referred to the end of this appendix, which contains a reproduction of the version of the questionnaire used in Dayton, Ohio. A slightly different version of the instrument was used in each city, the differences being confined entirely to the lists of specific productivity actions inserted in the first set of questions in each of the ten components of personnel management. A detailed list of the productivity actions by city is contained in appendix 2A.

Survey Methods

The survey was administered in person by three members of the professional staff of the Public Services Laboratory of Georgetown University over a 3-month period extending from December 1976 to March 1977. The staff spent 3 to 4 days in each of the cities administering the questionnaire to individual managers or small groups of managers. All three staff members participated in pilot administrations of the survey instrument in a suburban jurisdiction in the Washington, D.C. area, and all three participated in the administration of the survey instrument in the first city, Lakewood, to further standardize procedures. Two of the three staff members were present in four of the remaining seven cities, while only one person went to the other three cities.

In each city, initial arrangements were made for survey administration through the city representative to the research project. The selection of the productivity actions was made principally by the city representative in coordination with guidelines and some suggestions made by project staff. The guidelines were that there be a reasonable mix of projects, the projects be sufficiently broad as to be known to most of the managerial employees of the cities, that the projects had reached a reasonable stage of implementation, and that the projects had been undertaken fairly recently (within the last 2 or 3 years if possible). The city representative also participated in selecting the city managerial employees to be surveyed. Criteria for these decisions are discussed more fully in chapter 2.

After a mutually agreeable, 3- to 4-day period was picked for the survey administration, the city representative informed those city managerial employees who would be surveyed of the purposes of the study, the participation of the National League of Cities, U.S. Conference of Mayors, and Georgetown University, and arranged an interview schedule.

The survey was usually administered to small groups of people, from one to five in number, in a conference room in the city hall. Respondents filled out the questionnaire, with a researcher available to answer questions as needed. After a brief, standard introduction, they had as long as needed in one sitting to fill out the questionnaire. Most people took 45 minutes to 1 hour with the questionnaire. The oral introduction by the researchers emphasized several points which were listed in the introductory page of the questionnaire, including (1) the purpose of the study, (2) the participation of the National League of Cities and U.S. Conference of Mayors, along with the Public Services Laboratory of Georgetown University and the eight cities in the study, (3) the confidentiality of their responses, and (4) our interest in talking to them further after completion of the questionnaire.

We emphasized that their own city was interested in obtaining the candid assessment of its productivity actions in comparison with other cities. We also pointed out that the number code on each copy of the questionnaire was for analysis purposes only. Respondents were encouraged to answer every question they could, but they also were encouraged to answer "don't know" whenever appropriate. We did not want to force the respondents into uncomfortable situations—where they would have to make up an observation—and we believe that the reliability of the responses was improved by having allowed the respondents to decline to answer particular questions about which they had inadequate information. Finally, to make sure that the respondents knew exactly what was meant by each productivity action title, a separate one- to two-page sheet was handed out which described each productivity action in one paragraph. After the introductory speech, respondents were asked to read the introductory page of the survey and begin completing it.

The completed questionnaires were collected from the respondents before they left the interview site. In a few cases, respondents had to leave before completing the survey. In those cases, we provided our address and envelopes and asked them to mail the completed questionnaire to us at the earliest possible time. A copy of the survey instrument follows.

Productivity/Personnel Management Project

Conducted by Georgetown University, Public Services Laboratory
in conjunction with the League of Cities-Conference of Mayors, Inc.

Introduction

You have been selected to participate in a survey of city government employees about productivity and personnel management. The survey is the central research portion of an important study on how productivity and personnel decision making impact on one another.

Your city has agreed to participate in the project because the study will cover new ground and is expected to have a substantial payoff in insights and new directions toward more effective government. While productivity actions have been studied extensively in recent years, the linkages between personnel management and productivity have not. Yet, because people represent the greatest single resource of governments, the most significant productivity gains are likely to be achieved when these linkages are understood more fully so that the personnel management systems can be fully involved in productivity actions.

You as an individual were chosen for the survey because you are in a position to be knowledgeable about (1) one or more of the productivity-related actions that your city has undertaken and (2) the overall management framework of the city, particularly the management of people.

The survey is not seeking facts and figures. It is intended to obtain your best judgements—as an informed city employee—about the impact of the city's productivity actions and the factors that influence them. Your opinions are crucial to the results of the study.

Your Time. We realize how busy you are. The survey has been designed for ease of response. If you answer all the questions (and hopefully you can), you should not need more than an hour or so.

Confidentiality. Your responses to the survey questions will be kept in the strictest confidence. No individual respondent will be identified in the survey analysis or the project reports. Each respondent will be assigned a code number, solely to allow for comparisons between cities by categories of employees (such as personnel specialists). If you have any questions about the confidentiality of responses, don't hesitate to ask the Public Services Laboratory Staff.

114

Use of the Survey. The results of the survey will be used to identify important factors that influence the success of city productivity programs and ways in which the productivity actions impact on city management processes. Of special concern is the relationship between productivity and the ways that cities manage their personnel. The end product will be information useful to city leaders and employees on ways to manage personnel more effectively for greater productivity.

As mentioned earlier, your responses are crucial to the study. Large samples of city employees are not being surveyed. Instead, the project depends on smaller numbers of individually chosen employees to provide well informed opinions. Therefore, each response is highly important.

Format of the Survey. The survey is divided into ten brief sections, plus two general questions that conclude this introduction. The ten sections deal with the major components of personnel management and their relationship to your city's productivity actions. The emphasis in each of these sections is on determining your views on the impact of the component on implementation of your productivity actions. Less emphasis is placed on the reverse, that is, the impact of productivity upon the personnel management actions. For ease of completion, each section has questions that will allow you to determine whether your base of knowledge about the subject is sufficient to respond to follow-up questions. If not, the survey allows you simply to skip the follow-up questions.

The two general questions that conclude this introduction follow on the next page.

Thank you,

Public Services Laboratory Staff

1. Here is a list of the major productivity actions which have been implemented already or are being implemented now in your city. Please check the degree to which you believe the actions have affected the *quality* of your *city services.*

	Seriously Impeded	Slightly Impeded	No Impact	Slightly Helped	Greatly Helped	Don't Know
a. Management by objectives						
b. Reorganization of city administration						
c. Project management						
d. Centralized accounting						
e. Rerouting of waste collection						
f. Fire station location						
g. Geographic assignment of housing inspection						

2. Here is a list of offices and policies that may be involved in your city's productivity actions. In your judgment, what impact have these offices and policies had on the implementation of your productivity actions?

	Seriously Impeded	Slightly Impeded	No Impact	Slightly Helped	Greatly Helped	Don't Know
Mayor's office						
Council						
City manager or administrator						
City budget office						
City personnel office						
Department heads						
Employees organizations or unions						
Citizen groups						
Federal laws or regulations						
State laws or regulations						
City laws or regulations						
Other (please specify) _____						

Section I: Personnel Staffing Levels

The term *personnel staffing levels* is used in this section to mean the system or process of making *major* decisions on city program or department staffing levels. Because of the large impact of any major change in staff levels, these decisions generally will involve most or all of the top-level managers as well as your City Council and Mayor/Administrator.

Regardless of whether all of your top-level managers participate in the process of evaluating and/or changing program or department staffing levels, or whether the process is limited to a few individuals, it is important that you respond to the following questions in terms of the major staffing level decision-making process.

A. The Impact of Personnel Staffing-Level Decision Making
   on Productivity Efforts

1. The productivity actions listed below either have been or are being taken by your city government. Please check the degree to which you believe decisions on *personnel staffing levels* have affected the implementation of each productivity action.

	Seriously Impeded	Slightly Impeded	No Impact	Slightly Helped	Greatly Helped	Don't Know
a. Management by objectives						
b. Reorganization of city administration						
c. Project management						
d. Centralized accounting						
e. Rerouting of waste collection						
f. Fire station location						
g. Geographic assignment of housing inspection						

Note: If you checked any boxes in the previous question other than "Don't Know," please answer the following question (2). Otherwise, please skip question 2 and proceed to question 3.

2. Here is a list of factors (including individuals and offices) that may be involved in the process of deciding *personnel staffing levels*. In your judgment, what impact have those factors had (through staffing-level decisions) on the implementation of the city's productivity actions?

	Seriously Impeded	Slightly Impeded	No Impact	Slightly Helped	Greatly Helped	Don't Know
Fiscal policies						
Personnel rules and regulations						
EEO-Affirmative action guidelines						
Labor-management agreements						
City council						
Mayor						
City manager/administrator						
Budget director						
Personnel director						
Other (please specify) _____						

3. In terms of their involvement in the *personnel staffing level* decision-making process, which of the following programs or offices *could have provided* greater support for the implementation of your city's productivity actions?

	Yes	No	Don't Know
Fiscal policies			
Personnel rules and regulations			
EEO-Affirmative action guidelines			
Labor-management agreements			
City council			
Mayor			
City manager/administrator			
Budget director			
Personnel director			
Other (please specify) _____			

If you answered "yes" more than once, please circle the program or office which *could have made* the greatest contribution to the implementation of your productivity actions.

B. The Impact of Productivity Efforts on the Personnel Staffing-Level Decision-Making Process

1. Have any of your city's productivity actions resulted in changes in the *effectiveness* of decision-making on personnel staffing levels?

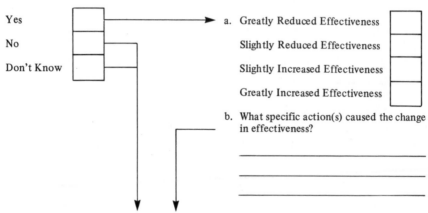

Yes

No

Don't Know

a. Greatly Reduced Effectiveness

Slightly Reduced Effectiveness

Slightly Increased Effectiveness

Greatly Increased Effectiveness

b. What specific action(s) caused the change in effectiveness?

_____

_____

_____

2. Have any of your city's productivity actions resulted in changes in the *cost* of decision-making on personnel staffing levels?

Yes

No

Don't Know

a. Greatly Reduced Cost

Slightly Reduced Cost

Slightly Increased Cost

Greatly Increased Cost

b. What specific action(s) caused the change in cost?

_____

_____

_____

Section II: Recruitment and Selection

This section concerns the *recruitment and selection* of city employees, that is, all the activities starting with reaching potential job applicants and ending with appointment of new employees. Recruitment and selection include such functions as preparing and distributing recruiting materials, operating job information centers, advertising jobs, visiting schools and other sources of applicants, examining and rating applicants, certifying eligible candidates, selecting candidates, and appointment. Regardless of where the recruitment and selection activities and decisions take place, it is important that you respond to the questions in terms of the complete process of recruitment and selection.

Note: In some cities, recruitment and selection may not be a relevant topic for study, due to the absence of recruiting activity. If in your judgment, the city has done no significant recruiting in the past year, please check the box below and proceed to Section III. Otherwise, please complete this section.

☐ No significant recruiting activity

A. *The Impact of the Recruiting and Selection Program on Productivity Actions*

1. The productivity actions listed below either have been or are being taken by your city government. Please check the degree to which you believe *recruiting and selection* have affected the implementation of each productivity action.

	Seriously Impeded	Slightly Impeded	No Impact	Slightly Helped	Greatly Helped	Don't Know
a. Management by objectives						
b. Reorganization of city administration						
c. Project management						
d. Centralized accounting						
e. Rerouting of waste collection						
f. Fire station location						
g. Geographic assignment of housing inspection						

Note: If you checked any boxes in the previous question other than "Don't Know," please answer the following question (2). Otherwise, please skip question 2 and proceed to question 3.

2. Here is a list of elements involved in the *recruiting and selection* process. In your judgment, what impact have these factors had on the implementation of your city's productivity actions?

	Seriously Impeded	Slightly Impeded	No Impact	Slightly Helped	Greatly Helped	Don't Know
Procedures for recruiting personnel						
Qualification of candidates produced by the recruiting efforts						
Selection standards, in relation to the qualifications required by productivity actions						
Selection devices/tests and procedures						
"Rule of three" or other similar selection rules						
Procedures for processing candidates for appointment						
Other (please specify) _____						

3. Which of the following *recruiting and selection* factors could have provided greater support for the implementation of your city's productivity actions?

	Yes	No	Don't Know
Procedures for recruiting personnel			
Qualifications of candidates produced by the recruiting efforts			
Selection standards, in relation to the qualifications required by productivity actions			
Selection devices/tests and procedures			
"Rule of three" or other similar selection rules			
Procedures for processing candidates for appointment			
Other (please specify) _____			

If you answered "yes" more than once, please circle the factor which *could have made* the greatest contribution to the implementation of your productivity actions.

B. *The Impact of Productivity Efforts on the Recruiting and Selection Process*

1. Have any of your city's productivity actions resulted in changes in the *effectiveness* of the *recruiting and selection* process.

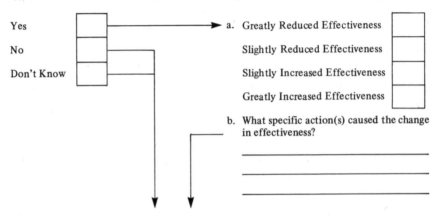

Yes

No

Don't Know

a. Greatly Reduced Effectiveness

Slightly Reduced Effectiveness

Slightly Increased Effectiveness

Greatly Increased Effectiveness

b. What specific action(s) caused the change in effectiveness?

_____

_____

_____

2. Have any of your city's productivity actions resulted in changes in the *cost* of the *recruiting and selection* process.

Yes

No

Don't Know

a. Greatly Reduced Cost

Slightly Reduced Cost

Slightly Increased Cost

Greatly Increased Cost

b. What specific action(s) caused the change in cost?

_____

_____

_____

Section III: Classification

The term *classification* is used to mean the system or process of evaluating jobs or positions and arranging them into occupational groups, classes, and grade levels on the basis of similarities of duties, responsibilities, and qualification requirements. A classification system may cover all city employees, or it may cover only certain segments of the employee population.

Regardless of whether your city's classification system is comprehensive or not, and regardless of where classification activities and decisions take place, it is important that you respond to the following questions in terms of the complete classification process.

A. The Impact of the Classification Program on Productivity Actions

1. The productivity actions listed below either have been or are being taken by your city government. Please check the degree to which you believe the *classification* system has affected the implementation of each productivity action.

	Seriously Impeded	Slightly Impeded	No Impact	Slightly Helped	Greatly Helped	Don't Know
a. Management by objectives						
b. Reorganization of city administration						
c. Project management						
d. Centralized accounting						
e. Rerouting of waste collection						
f. Fire station location						
g. Geographic assignment of housing inspection						

Note: If you checked any boxes in the previous question other than "Don't Know," please answer the following question (2). Otherwise, please skip question 2 and proceed to question 3.

2. Here is a list of elements involved in the *classification* process. In your judgment, what impact have these factors had on the implementation of your city's productivity actions?

	Seriously Impeded	Slightly Impeded	No Impact	Slightly Helped	Greatly Helped	Don't Know
Classification standards (the established criteria for use in classifying positions)						
Class specifications (the stated characteristics and qualifications requirements of groups of similar positions)						
Position descriptions (written in standard form and language)						
Procedures for getting positions classified properly						
Other (please specify) _____						

3. Which of the following *classification* factors could have provided greater support for the implementation of your city's productivity actions?

	Yes	No	Don't Know
Classification standards (the established criteria for use in classifying positions)			
Class specifications (the stated characteristics and qualifications requirements of groups of similar positions)			
Position descriptions (written in standard form and language)			
Procedures for getting positions classified properly			
Other (please specify) _____			

If you answered "yes" more than once, please circle the factor which *could have made* the greatest contribution to the implementation of your productivity actions.

*B. The Impact of Productivity Efforts on the
     Classification System*

1. Have any of your city's productivity actions resulted in changes in the *effectiveness* of the *classification* system.

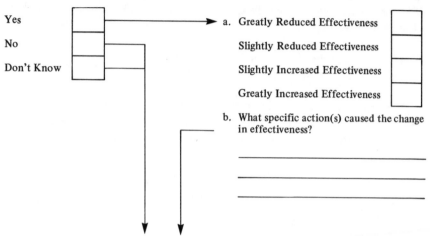

Yes

No

Don't Know

a. Greatly Reduced Effectiveness

Slightly Reduced Effectiveness

Slightly Increased Effectiveness

Greatly Increased Effectiveness

b. What specific action(s) caused the change in effectiveness?

_____

_____

_____

2. Have any of your city's productivity actions resulted in changes in the *cost* of the *classification* system.

Yes

No

Don't Know

a. Greatly Reduced Cost

Slightly Reduced Cost

Slightly Increased Cost

Greatly Increased Cost

b. What specific action(s) caused the change in cost?

_____

_____

_____

Section IV: Compensation

The term *compensation* is used to mean the city's plan or system of providing equitable salaries (pay) and benefits for its employees. Included are the statutory or regulatory bases for city salaries and benefits and such activities as a salary comparability survey and construction of a multiranged pay plan, cost-analysis of employee benefits (such as holidays and paid leave, health and life insurance, retirement, and the like)—all the functions which, taken together, make up the development, implementation, and maintenance of the total compensation system of the city.

Regardless of where decision affecting the compensation program take place, and regardless of who is responsible for actually conducting the program, it is important that you answer the questions in this section in terms of the complete compensation program.

A. The Impact of the Compensation Program on Productivity Actions

1. The productivity actions listed below have been or are being taken by your city government. Please check the degree to which you believe the *compensation* program has affected the implementation of each productivity action.

	Seriously Impeded	Slightly Impeded	No Impact	Slightly Helped	Greatly Helped	Don't Know
a. Management by objectives						
b. Reorganization of city administration						
c. Project management						
d. Centralized accounting						
e. Rerouting of waste collection						
f. Fire station location						
g. Geographic assignment of housing inspection						

Note: If you checked any boxes in the previous question other than "Don't Know," please answer the following question (2). Otherwise, please skip question 2 and proceed to question 3.

2. Here is a list of elements involved in *compensation*. In your judgment, what impact have these factors had on the implementation of your city's productivity actions?

	Seriously Impeded	Slightly Impeded	No Impact	Slightly Helped	Greatly Helped	Don't Know
Salaries and benefits as compared with those of private industry and other public employers						
Relationship of pay levels to the quantity, quality, and degree of difficulty of employees' outputs						
Procedures for establishing or changing pay levels						
Procedures for establishing or changing fringe benefits						
Policies and procedures for rewarding superior performance (through increased pay or benefits)						
Other (please specify) _____						

3. Which of the following *compensation* factors could have provided greater support for the implementation of your city's productivity actions?

	Yes	No	Don't Know
Salaries and benefits as compared with those of private industry and public employers			
Relationship of pay levels to the quantity, quality, and degree of difficulty of employees' outputs			
Procedures for establishing or changing pay levels			
Procedures for establishing or changing fringe benefits			
Policies and procedures for rewarding superior performance (through increased pay or benefits)			
Other (please specify) _____			

If you answered "yes" more than once, please circle the factor which *could have made* the greatest contribution to the implementation of your productivity actions.

B. *The Impact of Productivity Efforts on the Compensation Program*

1. Have any of your city's productivity actions resulted in changes in the *effectiveness* of the *compensation* program.

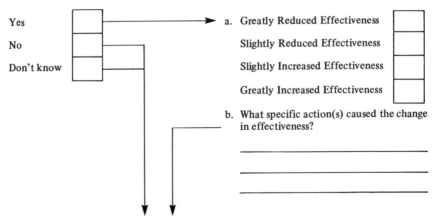

Yes

No

Don't know

a. Greatly Reduced Effectiveness

Slightly Reduced Effectiveness

Slightly Increased Effectiveness

Greatly Increased Effectiveness

b. What specific action(s) caused the change in effectiveness?

_____

_____

_____

2. Have any of your city's productivity actions resulted in changes in the *cost* of the *compensation* program.

Yes

No

Don't Know

a. Greatly Reduced Cost

Slightly Reduced Cost

Slightly Increased Cost

Greatly Increased Cost

b. What specific action(s) caused the change in cost?

_____

_____

_____

Section V: Performance Appraisal

The term *performance appraisal* is used to mean a program or system for regular, periodic evaluation of employees' job performance. Some fairly common types of performance appraisal are production record reviews, supervisors' rating scales, field reviews or audits, critical incident appraisals, essay appraisals, self evaluations, peer reviews, and subordinate appraisals.

Regardless of where decisions affecting the performance appraisal system take place and regardless of who is responsible for actually evaluating employees' performance, it is important that you answer the questions in this section in terms of the whole performance appraisal process.

Note: In some cities, the performance appraisal system may not be an appropriate subject for study, due to the absence of a system as such. It is assumed that managers in all cities are at some time involved in evaluating the performance of their employees, whether on an ad hoc, informal basis, or on a regular, periodic basis within the framework of an appraisal system. This section is concerned *only* with the latter. Therefore, if your city does *not* have a system under which employees are evaluated on a periodic basis and by use of some established method, please check the box below and proceed to Section VI. Otherwise, please complete this section.

☐ No formal performance appraisal system

A. The Impact of the Formal Performance Appraisal System on Productivity Actions

1. The productivity actions listed below either have been or are being taken by your city government. Please check the degree to which you believe the formal *performance appraisal* system has affected the implementation of each productivity action.

	Seriously Impeded	Slightly Impeded	No Impact	Slightly Helped	Greatly Helped	Don't Know
a. Management by objectives						
b. Reorganization of city administration						
c. Project management						
d. Centralized accounting						
e. Rerouting of waste collection						
f. Fire station location						
g. Geographic assignment of housing inspection						

Note: If you checked any boxes in the previous question other than "Don't Know," please answer the following question (2). Otherwise, please skip question 2 and proceed to question 3.

2. Here is a list of elements involved in the *performance appraisal* process. In your judgment, what impact have these factors had on the implementation of your city's productivity actions?

	Seriously Impeded	Slightly Impeded	No Impact	Slightly Helped	Greatly Helped	Don't Know
Coverage of the employee performance appraisal system (i.e., proportion of employees included)						
Procedures for evaluating employees' performance						
Policies or standards for identifying inadequate, acceptable, and superior performance						
Established methods of evaluating performance						
Other (please specify) _____						

3. Which of the following *performance appraisal* factors could have provided greater support for the implementation of your city's productivity actions?

	Yes	No	Don't Know
Coverage of the employee performance appraisal system (i.e., proportion of employees included)			
Procedures for evaluating employees' performance			
Policies or standards for identifying inadequate, acceptable, and superior performance			
Established methods of evaluating performance			
Other (please specify) _____			

If you answered "yes" more than once, please circle the factor which *could have made* the greatest contribution to the implementation of your productivity action.

B. *The Impact of Productivity Efforts on the Performance Appraisal System*

1. Have any of your city's productivity actions resulted in changes in the *effectiveness* of the *performance appraisal* system.

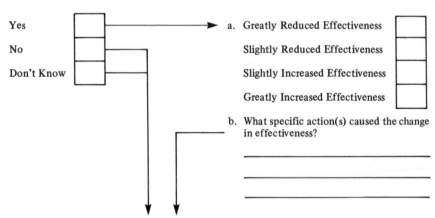

Yes

No

Don't Know

a. Greatly Reduced Effectiveness

Slightly Reduced Effectiveness

Slightly Increased Effectiveness

Greatly Increased Effectiveness

b. What specific action(s) caused the change in effectiveness?

_____

_____

_____

2. Have any of your city's productivity actions resulted in changes in the *cost* of the *performance appraisal* system.

Yes

No

Don't Know

a. Greatly Reduced Cost

Slightly Reduced Cost

Slightly Increased Cost

Greatly Increased Cost

b. What specific action(s) caused the change in cost?

_____

_____

_____

Section VI: Employee Development

The term *employee development* is used to mean a program of, or provisions for, enhancing employees' personal or career development through (1) training or instruction that is closely related to on-the-job application and is either provided or arranged by the city government and (2) other means such as short-term developmental assignments, planned increments of experience, and incentives for outside education (e.g., college or trade school programs), including approved absences from work and whole or partial tuition payments.

Regardless of where training decisions and activities take place, it is important that you respond to the following questions in terms of the entire process of employee development.

A. The Impact of the Employee Development Program on Productivity Actions

1. The productivity actions listed below either have been or are being taken by your city government. Please check the degree to which you believe the *employee development* program has affected the implementation of each productivity action.

	Seriously Impeded	Slightly Impeded	No Impact	Slightly Helped	Greatly Helped	Don't Know
a. Management by objectives						
b. Reorganization of city administration						
c. Project management						
d. Centralized accounting						
e. Rerouting of waste collection						
f. Fire station location						
g. Georgraphic assignment of housing inspection						

Note: If you checked any boxes in the previous question other than "Don't Know," please answer the following question (2). Otherwise, please skip question 2 and proceed to question 3.

2. Here is a list of elements involved in *employee development*. In your judgment, what impact have these factors had on the implementation of your city's productivity actions?

	Seriously Impeded	Slightly Impeded	No Impact	Slightly Helped	Greatly Helped	Don't Know
Coverage of formal employee development plan (i.e., proportion of employees included in a plan that identifies the specific training or developmental needs of employees)						
Procedures for identifying training needs						
Policies and procedures for obtaining training or developmental assignments for employees						
Policies or procedures for including training requirements in the planning for productivity-related actions						
Encouragements (such as liberal leave policies and tuition payments) for employees to obtain outside training or education						
Procedures for matching training to the actual needs of employees						
Other (please specify) _____						

3. Which of the following *employee development* factors could have provided greater support for the implementation of your city's productivity actions?

	Yes	No	Don't Know
Coverage of formal employee development plan (i.e., proportion of employees included in a plan that identifies the specific training or developmental needs of employees)			
Procedures for identifying training needs			
Policies and procedures for obtaining training or developmental assignments for employees			
Policies or procedures for including training requirements in the planning for productivity-related actions			
Encouragements (such as liberal leave policies and tuition payments) for employees to obtain outside training or education			
Procedures for matching training to the actual needs of employees			
Other (please specify) _____			

If you answered "yes" more than once, please circle the factor which *could have made* the greatest contribution to the implementation of your productivity actions.

B. The Impact of Productivity Efforts on the Employee Development Program

1. Have any of your city's productivity actions resulted in changes in the *effectiveness* of the *employee development* program.

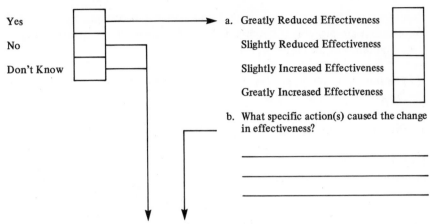

Yes
No
Don't Know

a. Greatly Reduced Effectiveness

Slightly Reduced Effectiveness

Slightly Increased Effectiveness

Greatly Increased Effectiveness

b. What specific action(s) caused the change in effectiveness?

_____

_____

_____

2. Have any of your city's productivity actions resulted in changes in the *cost* of the *employee development* program.

Yes

No

Don't Know

a. Greatly Reduced Cost

Slightly Reduced Cost

Slightly Increased Cost

Greatly Increased Cost

b. What specific action(s) caused the change in cost?

_____

_____

_____

Section VII: Promotions, Transfers, and Terminations

This section concerns the separate, but related processes of promoting, reassigning, and firing employees. Each of the processes includes statutory and/or regulatory bases for the personnel action, the criteria for determining who and when (i.e., who will be promoted and when), and the actual decisions to effect the personnel action.

In many cities, the rules governing personnel promotions, transfers, and terminations are included in a personnel statute. These may be expanded in regulations issued by the personnel office or a civil service commission. Sometimes, they may be affected by collective bargaining agreements. The case-by-case decisions on these personnel actions generally are left to individual managers and supervisors (frequently with some higher level review and approval required).

Regardless of where the various decisions about promotions, transfers, and terminations are made, it is important that you respond to the questions in this section in terms of the entire processes.

A. The Impact of the Promotion, Transfer, and Terminations Processes on Productivity Actions

1. The productivity actions listed below either have been or are being taken by your city government. Please check the degree to which you believe the formal *promotion, transfer, or termination* processes have affected the implementation of each productivity action.

	Seriously Impeded	Slightly Impeded	No Impact	Slightly Helped	Greatly Helped	Don't Know
a. Management by objectives						
b. Reorganization of city administration						
c. Project management						
d. Centralized accounting						
e. Rerouting of waste collection						
f. Fire station location						
g. Geographic assignment of housing inspection						

Note: If you checked any boxes in the previous question other than "Don't Know," please answer the following question (2). Otherwise, please skip question 2 and proceed to question 3.

2. Here is a list of elements involved in the *promotion, transfer, and termination* processes. In your judgment, what impact have these factors had on the implementation of your city's productivity actions?

	Seriously Impeded	Slightly Impeded	No Impact	Slightly Helped	Greatly Helped	Don't Know
Policies on considering employee performance in promotions and key lateral transfers						
Policies on considering seniority in promotions and key lateral transfers						
Time-in-grade (or similar) requirements for employees to be considered for promotions						
Policies and procedures for terminating employees "for cause"						
"last-hired, first-fired" (or similar) policies on terminations of employees during reductions-in-force						
Procedures for processing promotion, transfer and termination actions						
Other (please specify) _____						

3. Which of the following *promotion, transfer, and termination* factors could have provided greater support for the implementation of your city's productivity actions?

	Yes	No	Don't Know
Policies on considering employee performance in promotions and key lateral transfers			
Policies on considering seniority in promotions and key lateral transfers			
Time-in-grade (or similar) requirements for employees to be considered for promotions			
Policies and procedures for terminating employees "for cause"			
"Last-hired, first-fired" (or similar) policies on terminations of employees during reductions-in-force			
Procedures for processing promotion, transfer, and termination actions			
Other (please specify)			

If you answered "yes" more than once, please circle the factor which *could have made* the greatest contribution to the implementation of your productivity actions.

B. The Impact of Productivity Efforts on the Promotion, Transfer, and Terminations Processes

1. Have any of your city's productivity actions resulted in changes in the *effectiveness* of the *promotion, transfer, and termination* processes.

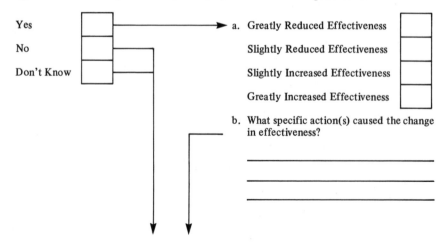

Yes

No

Don't Know

a. Greatly Reduced Effectiveness

Slightly Reduced Effectiveness

Slightly Increased Effectiveness

Greatly Increased Effectiveness

b. What specific action(s) caused the change in effectiveness?

_____

_____

_____

2. Have any of your city's productivity actions resulted in changes in the *cost* of the *promotions, transfers or terminations* processes.

Yes	☐
No	☐
Don't Know	☐

→

a. Greatly Reduced Cost ☐

   Slightly Reduced Cost ☐

   Slightly Increased Cost ☐

   Greatly Increased Cost ☐

b. What specific action(s) caused the change in cost?

_____

_____

_____

Section VIII: Employee-Employer Relations

The term *employee-employer relations* is used in this section to mean both the formal and informal exchanges of views and positions concerning productivity actions between management and employees. The consultations could involve individual employees as well as employee organizations and unions. The consultations could be either structured or unstructured and could take place from the initial planning phase for productivity actions through the development, implementation, operation, and final critique.

Regardless of where employee-employer relations activities take place, it is important that you respond to the following questions in terms of the full extent of the consultations on productivity taking place in your city.

A. The Impact of Employee-Employer Relations on Productivity Actions

1. The productivity actions listed below either have been or are being taken by your city government. Please check the degree to which you believe the *employee-employer relations* program (consultations on productivity actions only) has affected the implementation of each productivity action.

	Seriously Impeded	Slightly Impeded	No Impact	Slightly Helped	Greatly Helped	Don't Know
a. Management by objectives						
b. Reorganization of city administration						
c. Project management						
d. Centralized accounting						
e. Rerouting of waste collection						
f. Fire station location						
g. Geographic assignment of housing inspection						

Note: If you checked any boxes in the previous question other than "Don't Know," please answer the following question (2), Otherwise, please skip question 2 and proceed to question 3.

2. Here is a list of elements involved in *employee-employer relations.* In your judgment, what impact have these factors had on the implementation of your city's productivity actions?

	Seriously Impeded	Slightly Impeded	No Impact	Slightly Helped	Greatly Helped	Don't Know
Established procedures for management consultation with employees in the planning, development, and implementation of productivity actions						
Provisions for direct participation by employee representatives in the planning, development, and implementation of productivity actions						
Employee attitude toward consulting with management on planning, developing, or implementing productivity actions						
Management attitude toward consulting with employees on planning, developing or implementing productivity actions						
Other (please specify) _____						

3. Which of the following *employee-employer relations* factors could have provided greater support for the implementation of your city's productivity actions?

	Yes	No	Don't Know
Established procedure for management consultation with employees in the planning, development, and implementation of productivity actions			
Provisions for direct participation by employee representatives in the planning, development, and implementation of productivity actions			
Employee attitude toward consulting with management on planning, developing, or implementing productivity actions			
Management attitude toward consulting with employees on planning, developing, or implementing productivity actions			
Other (please specify) _____			

If you answered "yes" more than once, please circle the factor which *could have made* the greatest contribution to the implementation of your productivity actions.

B. The Impact of Productivity Efforts on the Employee-Employer Relations Program

1. Have any of your city's productivity actions resulted in changes in the *effectiveness* of the *employee-employer relations* program.

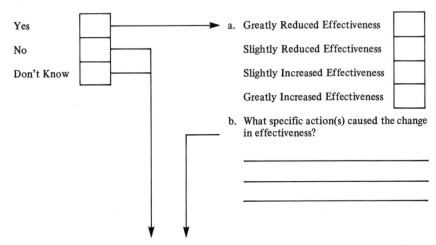

Yes

No

Don't Know

a. Greatly Reduced Effectiveness

Slightly Reduced Effectiveness

Slightly Increased Effectiveness

Greatly Increased Effectiveness

b. What specific action(s) caused the change in effectiveness?

_____

_____

_____

2. Have any of your city's productivity actions resulted in changes in the *cost* of the *employee-employer relations* program.

Yes ☐ ⟶ a. Greatly Reduced Cost ☐

No ☐   Slightly Reduced Cost ☐

Don't Know ☐   Slightly Increased Cost ☐

     Greatly Increased Cost ☐

     b. What specific action(s) caused the change in cost?

_____

_____

_____

Section IX: Collective Bargaining

This section concerns management's involvement in the *collective bargaining* process, that is, all the activities within the city government related to obtaining and supporting the contracts or work agreements between the city and employee unions and organizations concerning the services of city employees. Collective bargaining includes such functions as conducting talks and formal negotiations of contracts with unions and/or employee organizations, handling day-to-day dealings with their representatives on contract issues, administration of the contracts, conducting research and staff support for talks and formal negotiations, and administration of the formal grievance procedure.

Regardless of where the collective bargaining activities take place, it is important that you respond to the questions in terms of the overall management role in the collective bargaining process.

Note: In some cities, employees may not be organized, or may not engage in collective bargaining activities. If this is the case in your city, please check the box below and proceed to Section X. Otherwise, please complete this section.

☐ No significant collective bargaining activities

A. The Impact of the Collective Bargaining Process on Productivity Actions

1. The productivity actions listed below either have been or are being taken by your city government. Please check the degree to which you believe the *collective bargaining* process has affected the implementation of each productivity action.

	Seriously Impeded	Slightly Impeded	No Impact	Slightly Helped	Greatly Helped	Don't Know
a. Management by objectives						
b. Reorganization of city administration						
c. Project management						
d. Centralized accounting						
e. Rerouting of waste collection						
f. Fire station location						
g. Geographic assignment of housing inspection						

Note: If you checked any boxes in the previous question other than "Don't Know," please answer the following question (2). Otherwise, please skip question 2 and proceed to question 3.

2. Here is a list of elements involved in the *collective bargaining* process. In your judgment, what impact have these factors had on the implementation of your city's productivity actions?

	Seriously Impeded	Slightly Impeded	No Impact	Slightly Helped	Greatly Helped	Don't Know
Labor-management agreement provisions relating to worker productivity						
Number of separate bargaining units						
Attitude of unions or employee organizations toward productivity as a bargaining issue						
Attitude of management toward productivity as a bargaining issue						
Procedures for the bargaining process						
Grievance procedures						
Other (please specify)_____						

3. Which of the following *collective bargaining* process factors could have provided greater support for the implementation of your city's productivity actions?

	Yes	No	Don't Know
Labor-management agreement provisions relating to worker productivity			
Number of separate bargaining units			
Attitude of unions or employee organizations toward productivity as a bargaining issue			
Attitude of management toward productivity as a bargaining issue			
Procedures for the bargaining process			
Grievance procedures			
Other (please specify) _____			

If you answered "yes" more than once, please circle the factors which *could have made* the greatest contribution to the implementation of your productivity actions.

B. The Impact of Productivity Efforts on the Collective Bargaining Process

1. Have any of your city's productivity actions resulted in changes in the *effectiveness* of the *collective bargaining* process.

Yes

No

Don't Know

a. Greatly Reduced Effectiveness

Slightly Reduced Effectiveness

Slightly Increased Effectiveness

Greatly Increased Effectiveness

b. What specific action(s) caused the change in effectiveness?

_____

_____

_____

2. Have any of your city's productivity actions resulted in changes in the *cost* of the *collective bargaining* process.

Yes [ ] ⟶ a. Greatly Reduced Cost [ ]

No [ ]   Slightly Reduced Cost [ ]

Don't Know [ ]   Slightly Increased Cost [ ]

                 Greatly Increased Cost [ ]

b. What specific action(s) caused the change in cost?

_____

_____

_____

Section X: EEO-Affirmative Action

This section concerns the city's EEO-Affirmative Action program, that is, all the activities related to establishing and enforcing antidiscrimination policies, as well as establishing and implementing Affirmative Action guidelines or quotas.

Regardless of where the EEO-Affirmative Action activities take place, it is important that you respond to the questions in terms of the overall management role in the EEO-Affirmative Action program.

Note: In some cities, EEO-Affirmative Action may not be a relevant topic for study, due to the absence of significant activity in the area. If in your judgment the city has no significant ongoing EEO-Affirmative Action program, please check the box below and return this form to your interviewer or monitor. Otherwise, please compete this section.

[ ] No Significant EEO-Affirmative Action Activities

A. The Impact of the EEO-Affirmative Action Program on Productivity Actions

1. The productivity actions listed below either have been or are being taken by your city government. Please check the degree to which you believe the *EEO-Affirmative Action* program has affected the implementation of each productivity action.

	Seriously Impeded	Alightly Impeded	No Impact	Slightly Helped	Greatly Helped	Don't Know
a. Management by objectives						
b. Reorganization of city administration						
c. Project management						
d. Centralized accounting						
e. Rerouting of waste collection						
f. Fire station location						
g. Geographic assignment of housing inspection						

Note: If you checked any boxes in the previous question other than "Don't Know," please answer the following question (2). Otherwise, please skip question 2 and proceed to question 3.

2. Here is a list of elements involved in the *EEO-Affirmative Action* program. In your judgment, what impact have these factors had on the implementation of your city's productivity actions?

	Seriously Impeded	Slightly Impeded	No Impact	Slightly Helped	Greatly Helped	Don't Know
EEO antidiscrimination policies and procedures						
Affirmative action guidelines						
Hiring and/or promotion quotas						
EEO-Affirmative action appeal or complaint procedures						
Other (please specify)						

3. Which of the following *EEO-Affirmative Action* program factors could have provided greater support for the implementation of your city's productivity actions?

	Yes	No	Don't Know
EEO antidiscrimination policies and procedures			
Affirmative Action guidelines			
Hiring and/or promotion quotas			
EEO-Affirmative Action appeal of complaint procedures			
Other (please specify) _____			

If you answered "yes" more than once, please circle the factor which *could have made* the greatest contribution to the implementation of your productivity actions.

B. The Impact of Productivity Efforts on the EEO-Affirmative Action Program

1. Have any of your city's productivity actions resulted in changes in the *effectiveness* of the *EEO-Affirmative Action* program.

Yes ☐ ⟶ a. Greatly Reduced Effectiveness ☐

No ☐   Slightly Reduced Effectiveness ☐

Don't Know ☐   Slightly Increased Effectiveness ☐

Greatly Increased Effectiveness ☐

b. What specific action(s) caused the change in effectiveness?

_____

_____

_____

2. Have any of your city's productivity actions resulted in changes in the *cost* of the *EEO-Affirmative Action* program.

Yes [ ] ⟶ a. Greatly Reduced Cost [ ]

No [ ]   Slightly Reduced Cost [ ]

Don't Know [ ]   Slightly Increased Cost [ ]

Greatly Increased Cost [ ]

b. What specific action(s) caused the change in cost?

_____

_____

_____

Appendix B
Further Results

This appendix reports further details on the survey results. The primary focus is to provide city-by-city results for those factors of personnel management which stand out as either impeding or helping the implementation of productivity actions, and to report aggregate data in tabular form which was not reported in chapter 2 of this book. The purpose of reporting these data is to further illustrate the variations among the eight cities and indicate the extent to which cross-city generalizations are valid. A final section of this appendix reports further information on the distribution of sample respondents and "don't know" responses.

City-by-City Results

Table B-1 reports data on a city-by-city basis analogous to that in table 2-3. Although there are individual variations by city, the general pattern seems to hold that factors within the classification, promotions, transfers and terminations, and compensation components were the greatest impediments to implementing productivity actions. The greatest support comes from employee development, performance appraisal, and employer-employee relations. Interestingly enough, in five of the cities EEO-Affirmative Action programs are generally agreed to have had no impact on productivity improvements, while in the other three, St. Paul, Scottsdale, and Tacoma, over 40 percent of the respondents thought EEO programs and policies had impeded productivity implementation.

Compared with the cross-city averages, the most unusual of these cities is Lakewood. The average percentage response in the impeded category in Lakewood is substantially smaller than for other cities, and the corresponding percentage of responses in the helped category is substantially higher. Particularly striking differences occur in Lakewood in the low percentages of responses in the impeded category for the recruitment and selection and promotions, transfers, and terminations categories. Perhaps these responses reflect the relatively heavy emphasis in Lakewood on innovative techniques and systematic analysis of objectives, goals, and options. However, these ratings may reflect the comparative newness of the city and its relatively small size. The other two smallest cities in this survey, Scottsdale and Savannah, also had relatively low percentages in the impeded category.

Table B-2 reports distributions by city for seven specific factors within the nine personnel components that were judged to be impediments. Comparable

Table B-1
Overall Impact of Personnel Management Components Based on Averaging Responses to the Factors within Each Component

Personnel Management Component	Dayton			Lakewood			Nashville			St. Paul		
	Impeded	No Impact	Helped	Impeded	No Impact	Helped	Impeded	No Impact	Helped	Impeded	No Impact	Helped
Recruitment and selection	43.6%	32.3%	24.2%	9.2%	31.0%	59.8%	36.3%	31.3%	32.5%	40.7%	24.4%	34.9%
Classification	27.7	15.4	56.9	42.6	24.6	32.8	38.7	30.7	30.7	37.7	11.6	50.7
Compensation	37.5	22.7	39.8	23.5	6.2	70.4	41.4	24.1	34.5	36.0	43.8	20.2
Performance appraisal	25.8	8.1	66.1	3.0	7.6	89.4	19.4	28.4	52.2	23.2	25.0	51.8
Employee development	19.6	21.7	58.7	30.3	19.1	50.6	26.2	17.8	56.1	5.4	40.2	54.4
Promotions, transfers, terminations	54.7	24.4	20.9	17.7	38.0	44.3	36.3	38.2	25.5	51.6	21.5	26.9
Employee-employer relations	36.9	21.5	41.5	29.3	1.7	69.0	23.7	23.7	52.5	25.9	18.5	55.6
Collective bargaining	47.7	30.2	22.1	25.0	34.1	40.9	14.0	56.1	20.9	55.9	36.6	7.5
EEO-Affirmative Action	16.4	61.8	21.8	8.7	65.2	26.1	31.8	54.6	13.6	49.2	49.2	1.6
Average	34.4	26.5	39.1	21.0	25.3	53.7	29.8	34.9	35.4	36.2	30.1	33.7

Personnel Management Component	Savannah			Scottsdale			Tacoma			Worcester		
	Impeded	No Impact	Helped	Impeded	No Impact	Helped	Impeded	No Impact	Helped	Impeded	No Impact	Helped
Recruitment and selection	30.3%	22.5%	47.2%	22.7%	26.1%	51.1%	42.0%	25.9%	32.1%	32.8%	19.4%	47.8%
Classification	27.6	25.9	46.6	32.8	25.4	41.8	40.5	38.9	20.6	29.4	23.5	47.1
Compensation	49.3	14.1	36.6	22.7	17.3	60.0	39.3	37.2	23.5	58.6	27.1	14.3
Performance appraisal	30.4	4.4	65.2	25.9	6.9	67.2	38.6	45.7	15.7	23.5	26.5	50.0
Employee development	16.3	20.0	63.8	13.5	16.9	69.7	9.6	21.1	69.4	23.4	14.3	62.3
Promotions, transfers, terminations	29.5	47.4	23.1	25.0	47.9	27.1	35.3	50.5	14.2	42.7	28.0	29.3
Employee-employer relations	40.0	42.0	18.0	32.1	23.2	44.6	23.9	11.5	64.6	17.0	17.0	66.0
Collective bargaining	12.1	69.0	19.0	—	—	—	48.3	18.2	33.6	55.2	27.6	17.2
EEO-Affirmative Action	25.4	54.2	20.3	41.7	53.3	5.0	42.5	32.5	25.0	21.1	55.3	23.7
Average	29.0	33.3	37.8	27.1	27.1	45.8	35.6	31.3	33.2	33.7	26.5	39.7

Note: The distributions reported in this table represent the averages of respondents' ratings of the impact on productivity actions in general of four to seven specific factors within each personnel component.

Table B-2
Impediments: Percentage Distribution of Responses to Seven Personnel Management Factors

	Dayton			Lakewood			Nashville			St. Paul		
	Impeded	No Impact	Helped	Impeded	No Impact	Helped	Impeded	No Impact	Helped	Impeded	No Impact	Helped
1. Procedures for getting positions classified properly	47.1%	5.9%	47.1%	50.0%	18.8%	31.3%	57.9%	15.8%	26.3%	52.9%	11.8%	35.3%
2. Procedures for establishing or changing pay levels	47.1	11.7	41.2	35.3	5.9	58.8	47.4	21.1	31.6	61.1	27.8	11.1
3. Policies and procedures for rewarding superior performance (through increased pay or benefits)	31.6	42.1	26.3	12.5	–	87.5	52.9	23.5	23.5	41.2	58.8	–
4. Policies and procedures for terminating employees "for cause"	62.5	18.8	18.8	42.9	7.1	50.0	43.8	25.0	31.3	46.7	26.7	26.7
5. Procedures for processing promotion, transfer, and termination actions	56.3	25.0	18.8	15.4	30.8	53.9	47.4	31.6	21.1	66.7	6.7	26.7
6. Number of separate bargaining units (collective bargaining)	71.4	21.4	7.1	12.5	62.5	25.0	–	71.4	28.6	75.0	25.0	–
7. Attitude of unions or employee organizations toward productivity as a bargaining issue	78.6	14.3	7.1	42.9	42.9	14.3	28.6	42.9	28.6	68.8	31.3	–

	Savannah			Scottsdale			Tacoma			Worcester		
	Impeded	No Impact	Helped	Impeded	No Impact	Helped	Impeded	No Impact	Helped	Impeded	No Impact	Helped
1. Procedures for getting positions classified properly	30.8%	15.4%	53.9%	41.2%	23.5%	35.3%	56.7%	26.7%	16.7%	30.8%	15.4%	53.9%
2. Procedures for establishing or changing pay levels	60.0	–	40.0	28.6	14.3	57.1	50.0	33.3	16.7	57.1	28.6	14.3
3. Policies and procedures for rewarding superior performance (through increased pay or benefits)	53.9	30.8	15.4	33.3	13.3	53.3	50.0	41.7	8.3	78.6	21.4	–
4. Policies and procedures for terminating employees "for cause"	46.7	26.7	26.7	47.0	23.5	29.4	35.5	54.8	9.7	30.8	38.4	30.8
5. Procedures for processing promotion, transfer, and termination actions	30.8	38.5	30.8	31.3	43.8	25.0	38.7	48.4	12.9	33.3	8.3	58.3
6. Number of separate bargaining units (collective bargaining)	–	100.0	–	–	–	–	80.8	15.4	3.9	66.7	22.2	11.1
7. Attitude of unions or employee organizations toward productivity as a bargaining issue	20.0	60.0	20.0	–	–	–	63.6	9.1	27.3	83.3	16.7	–

Note: The distributions reported in this table represent the averages of respondents' ratings of the impact on productivity actions in general of each of the specific factors listed.

distributions, aggregated across all eight cities, are reported in table 2-4. Again, there are city-specific variations around the aggregate averages, but the general pattern holds fairly well in most of the eight cities. The principal exception is Lakewood. The extent to which these factors impeded the implementation of productivity actions in Lakewood is relatively smaller than in the other seven cities, probably reflecting less comprehensive and rigid civil service rules. Apparently Lakewood has been more flexible in rewarding superior performance with pay as well as promotions and transfers.

Several of the cities, Nashville, Scottsdale, Savannah, and Lakewood, have had relatively little difficulty with the number of collective bargaining units or the attitude of employee groups or unions toward productivity. This is so because unions are nonexistent or relatively weak in their areas. In contrast, the other four cities have a fairly high degree of consensus, 63.6 to 83.3 percent, that these factors have impeded the implementation of productivity improvements.

The other city-by-city differences in the extent to which these factors impeded productivity improvements apparently are fairly small except for two, which probably reflect particular circumstances in the cities. Rewarding superior performance was not rated as a significant impeding factor in Dayton, perhaps because a new system of rewarding department managers based on performance had recently been implemented. It was surprising that the managers in Worcester did not consider the procedures for getting positions classified as more of an impediment, given their statewide civil service system. One possible explanation is that Worcester has less trouble than other cities in Massachusetts because of wider delegation of authority to Worcester than to other cities.

There are even fewer differences among the eight cities on the aspects of personnel management which support productivity improvement than there are on the impediments. Table B-3 reports the distributions of responses on a city-by-city basis for the same factors in the supporting components of personnel management reported on an aggregated basis in table 2-6. Examination of the performance appraisal section reveals that for seven of the eight cities, the consensus was widespread that all four of the factors in performance appraisal helped productivity actions. Of the twenty-eight distributions (four factors in each of seven cities), twenty-five have 50 percent or more of the responses in the helped category. The other three distributions have more than 40 percent in the helped category. Among these seven cities, Lakewood stands out in the near unanimity of opinion on the positive impact of performance appraisal, with 89 percent in the helped category, while three of the other six cities are grouped around 66 percent and the other three cities are grouped around 50 percent. The difference between these two groups of cities, as well as the difference between them and Lakewood, is probably related mainly to the performance appraisal techniques in use and coverage of performance appraisal in the cities. In the eighth city, Tacoma, there was consensus that performance appraisal has not helped productivity improvement.

Consensus on the impact of various factors in employee development is more consistent across the eight cities than for performance appraisal. The city averages for this component range from 50.8 to 69.1 percent in the helped category. There was somewhat more variation within cities, however. Specifically, less than a third of the respondents in Worcester and Nashville indicated that encouragement for employees to obtain outside training, such as liberal leave or tuition payments, had helped the implementation of productivity actions. This probably reflects the relative lack of such encouragements in these cities.

Consensus on the positive impact of employee-employer relations, formal and informal, is also relatively uniform across seven of the eight cities. The exception is Savannah, where there are very limited established provisions for employee representatives in planning, developing, or implementing productivity actions. The employees' attitudes toward consultation, in the opinions of the managers, have not helped.

Other Aggregate Results

In this section, the distributions of responses to the various parts of questions 2 and 3 of the questionnaire are reported in tabular form. Further results are not reported on questions 1 and 4 for reasons detailed below.

In question 1 of each section of the questionnaire, the city employees were asked to assess the impact of the nine personnel management components on the implementation of each of the specific productivity actions in the cities. The distribution of responses, aggregating across productivity actions and across cities, is reported in chapter 2 (table 2-2). After considerable effort to aggregate the responses into categories of productivity action, we concluded that there is more variation in the distribution of responses within a category than between categories. Moreover, the variations seemed to reflect particular aspects of the implementation of the specific productivity actions rather than generalized phenomena. This, combined with the larger share of responses in the "no impact" category when the broader components of personnel management are used and the large number of individual productivity actions, lead us not to report the distribution of responses by individual productivity action.

Results from question 4 (labeled as Part B on the questionnaire) are also not reported. This section asked respondents to consider the impact of the productivity actions on the various components of personnel management, that is, the converse of the impacts that were asked about in the first three questions. Examination of the responses to open-ended questions contained in this part of this questionnaire, as well as the verbal comments of respondents, lead us to conclude that these questions were not accurately interpreted by the respondents. Since the results would be misleading at best, they are not reported.

Table B-3
Supports: Percentage Distribution of Responses about Three Personnel Management Components

	Dayton			Lakewood			Nashville		
	Impeded	No Impact	Helped	Impeded	No Impact	Helped	Impeded	No Impact	Helped
Performance Appraisal:									
Coverage of the employee performance appraisal system (i.e., proportion of employees included)	33.3%	13.3%	53.3%	–	25.0%	75.0%	–	42.9%	57.1%
Procedures for evaluating employees' performance	29.4	11.8	58.8	–	–	100.0	15.8%	31.6	52.6
Policies or standards for identifying inadequate, acceptable, and superior performance	20.0	–	80.0	11.8%	5.9	82.4	29.4	17.7	52.9
Established methods of evaluating performance	20.0	6.7	73.3	–	–	100.0	29.4	23.5	47.1
Average	25.7	8.0	66.4	3.0	7.7	89.4	18.7	28.9	52.4
Employee Development:									
Coverage of formal employee development plan (i.e., proportion of employees included in a plan that identifies the specific training or developmental needs of employees)	25.0	25.0	50.0	35.7	14.3	50.0	26.7	13.3	60.0
Procedures for identifying training needs	20.0	20.0	60.0	37.5	18.6	43.8	20.0	20.0	60.0
Policies and procedures for obtaining training or developmental assignments for employees	25.0	12.5	62.5	33.3	20.0	46.7	23.5	5.9	70.6
Policies or procedures for including training requirements in the planning for productivity-related actions	28.6	28.6	42.9	31.3	18.8	50.0	22.2	5.6	72.2
Encouragements (such as liberal leave policies and tuition payments) for employees to obtain outside training or education	–	17.7	82.4	21.4	14.3	64.3	27.8	38.9	33.3
Procedures for matching training to the actual needs of employees	21.4	28.6	50.0	21.4	28.6	50.0	36.8	21.1	42.1
Average	20.0	22.1	58.0	30.1	19.1	50.8	26.2	17.5	56.4
Employee-Employer Relations:									
Established procedures for management consultation with employees in the planning, development, and implementation of productivity actions	27.8	27.8	44.4	26.7	–	73.3	12.5	31.3	56.3
Provisions for direct participation by employee representatives in the planning, development, and implementation of productivity actions	29.4	35.3	35.3	28.6	7.1	64.3	14.3	35.7	50.0
Employee attitude toward consulting with management on planning, developing, or implementing productivity actions	46.7	13.3	40.0	33.3	–	66.7	28.6	28.6	42.9
Management attitude toward consulting with employees on planning, developing, or implementing productivity actions	46.7	6.7	46.7	28.6	–	71.4	40.0	–	60.0
Average	37.7	20.8	41.6	29.3	1.8	68.9	23.9	23.9	52.3

Note: The distributions reported in this table represent the averages of respondents' ratings of the impact on productivity actions in general of each of the specific factors listed.

	St. Paul			Savannah			Scottsdale			Tacoma			Worcester	
Impeded	No Impact	Helped	Impeded	No Impact	Helped	Impeded	No Impact	Helped	Impeded	No Impact	Helped	Impeded	No Impact	Helped
7.1%	35.7%	57.1%	33.3%	16.7%	50.0%	—	15.4%	84.6%	23.5%	58.8%	17.7%	33.3%	16.7%	50.0%
26.7	20.0	53.3	20.0	—	80.0	33.3%	—	66.7	42.1	42.1	15.8	22.2	33.3	44.4
35.7	21.4	42.9	33.3	—	66.7	33.3	6.7	60.0	41.2	41.2	17.7	20.0	30.0	50.0
23.1	23.1	53.9	33.3	—	66.7	33.3	6.7	60.0	47.1	41.2	11.8	20.0	30.0	50.0
23.2	25.1	51.8	30.0	4.2	65.9	25.0	7.2	67.8	38.5	45.8	15.8	23.9	27.5	48.6
8.3	50.0	41.7	23.1	15.4	61.5	—	26.7	73.3	6.7	23.3	70.0	25.0	8.3	66.7
5.9	35.3	58.8	15.4	7.7	76.9	13.3	13.3	73.3	8.8	17.7	73.5	21.4	7.1	71.4
5.9	35.3	58.8	21.4	21.4	57.1	26.7	6.7	66.7	9.7	19.4	71.0	15.4	7.7	76.9
6.7	46.7	46.7	14.3	21.4	64.3	20.0	20.0	60.0	3.5	31.0	65.5	15.4	23.1	61.5
—	37.5	62.5	7.1	42.9	50.0	6.3	6.3	87.5	12.9	32.3	54.8	38.5	30.8	30.8
6.7	40.0	53.3	16.7	8.3	75.0	15.4	30.8	53.9	17.7	11.8	70.6	25.0	8.3	66.7
5.6	40.8	53.6	16.3	19.5	64.1	13.6	17.3	69.1	9.9	22.6	67.6	23.5	14.2	62.3
15.4	23.1	61.5	28.6	42.9	28.6	42.9	14.3	42.9	13.3	23.3	63.3	15.4	23.1	61.5
23.1	30.8	46.2	27.3	63.6	9.1	28.6	28.6	42.9	15.1	6.1	78.8	9.1	18.2	72.7
35.7	7.1	57.1	50.0	41.7	8.3	35.7	28.6	35.7	30.3	12.1	57.6	14.3	14.3	71.4
28.6	14.3	57.1	53.9	23.1	23.1	21.4	21.4	57.1	35.3	5.9	58.8	26.7	13.3	60.0
25.7	18.8	55.5	32.9	42.8	17.3	32.2	23.2	44.7	23.5	11.9	64.6	16.4	17.2	66.4

The second question in the survey asked the respondents to assess the impact of various specific factors within the nine components of personnel management on the implementation of productivity actions. Complete data from three of the nine components, the strongest supports for productivity improvement, are reported in chapter 2 (table 2-6). Table B-4 reports the other six components of personnel management (from which the fourteen impediments and likely impediments in tables 2-4 and 2-5 were identified). Since the impeding factors contained in these six components have been discussed in chapter 2, the discussion that follows concentrates on those additional factors which are viewed as supports for productivity improvement.

The recruitment process seems, on balance, to have supported productivity implementation. Three of the six factors within recruitment and selection (recruiting procedures, qualifications of candidates, and selection standards) received positive assessments by approximately 50 percent of the respondents but negative assessments by 30 percent. What is interesting about these three factors is the relatively low number of responses in "no impact" and, therefore, the sharp division between those who responded "impeded" and those who responded "helped." This may reflect the relative lack of flexibility in classification and pay levels relative to the private sector. That is, managers whose departments employ people with highly paid private employment opportunities may be frustrated about their lack of success in recruiting, while other managers, whose employees may not have attractive alternatives in private industry, may consider recruitment as successful.

The same sharp division between impeded and helped is observed for the procedures for getting positions classified properly in the classification component, further supporting this interpretation. The other factors in classification are marginally on the helped side of the ledger, though with substantial representation in the "no impact" and "impeded" response categories.

Three of the five factors in compensation have already been discussed as impeding factors. Another interesting factor, "salaries and benefits as compared with those of private industry and other public employers," again elicited a strong split in the responses. While 53.5 percent indicated this comparison had helped, only 15.3 percent responded "no impact," and 31.2 percent perceived it as an impediment to productivity actions. This too supports the interpretation of restrictive rules, but also, importantly, indicates that in general the respondents do not consider local government salary levels to be too low to attract the appropriate labor force. These results suggest that the distribution of salary levels may be overly concentrated in city governments, too high for the least skilled and too low for the highly skilled.

Four of the six factors in the promotions, transfers, and terminations component have previously been discussed as impediments to the implementation of productivity actions. One of the other factors, "policies on considering employee performance in promotions and key lateral transfers," elicited a

Table B-4

Distribution of Responses for Six Components of Personnel Management

	Impeded	No Impact	Helped
Recruitment and Selection:			
Procedures for recruiting personnel	33.6 %	18.2 %	48.1 %
Qualifications of candidates produced by the recruiting efforts	28.8	16.5	54.6
Selection standards, in relation to the qualifications required by productivity actions	30.0	21.5	48.5
Selection devices/tests and procedures	31.1	28.9	40.0
"Rule of three" or other similar selection rules	32.3	47.0	20.6
Procedures for processing candidates for appointment	28.8	32.0	39.2
Average	30.77	27.35	41.83
Classification:			
Classification standards (the established criteria for use in classifying positions)	31.8	24.0	44.2
Class specifications (the stated characteristics and qualifications requirements of groups of similar positions)	34.3	26.5	39.2
Position descriptions (written in standard form and language)	26.5	30.1	43.3
Procedures for getting positions classified properly	45.9	17.3	36.8
Average	34.62	24.48	40.88
Compensation:			
Salaries and benefits as compared with those of private industry and other public employers	31.2	15.3	53.5
Relationship of pay levels to the quantity, quality, and degree of difficulty of employees' outputs	35.5	22.1	42.5
Procedures for establishing or changing pay levels	48.2	18.1	33.7
Procedures for establishing or changing fringe benefits	33.6	38.1	28.2
Policies and procedures for rewarding superior performance (through increased pay or benefits)	43.5	28.7	27.8
Average	38.40	24.46	37.14
Promotion, Transfer, and Termination:			
Policies on considering employee performance in promotions and key lateral transfers	31.0	20.3	48.6
Policies on considering seniority in promotions and key lateral transfers	36.1	41.8	22.2
Time-in-grade (or similar) requirements for employees to be considered for promotions	34.2	47.6	18.2

Table B-4   (Continued)

	Impeded	No Impact	Helped
Promotion, Transfer, and Termination: (Continued)			
Policies and procedures for terminating employees "for cause"	44.4. %	27.6 %	28.0 %
"Last-hired, first-fired" (or similar) policies on terminations of employees during reductions-in-force	32.2	60.8	7.0
Procedures for processing promotion, transfer, and termination actions	39.8	29.5	30.6
Average	36.28	37.93	25.77
Collective Bargaining:			
Labor-management agreement provisions relating to worker productivity	32.2	42.7	25.1
Number of separate bargaining units	52.2	38.9	8.9
Attitude of unions or employee organizations toward productivity as a bargaining issue	60.8	27.8	11.4
Attitude of management toward productivity as a bargaining issue	26.6	35.6	37.8
Procedures for the bargaining process	35.4	40.7	23.9
Grievance procedures	34.6	37.0	28.4
Average	40.3	37.12	22.58
EEO-Affirmative Action:			
EEO antidiscrimination policies and procedures	28.7	49.7	21.6
Affirmative Action guidelines	23.5	50.9	25.6
Hiring and/or promotion quotas	34.4	56.0	9.7
EEO-Affirmative Action appeal or complaint procedures	36.2	56.3	7.5
Average	30.7	53.22	16.1

Note: The other three components are reported in table 2-6. The raw data are the responses to question 2 of the survey. Percentages are weighted averages in which each individual response is weighted in inverse proportion to the total number of responses from that city. "Don't know" responses were deleted from the computation of distributions.

dichotomous response, with 40 percent indicating "helped" and 31 percent indicating "impeded." Since one normally would expect such policies to help productivity actions, to the extent they are implemented, the 31 percent impeded seems to imply that such policies are not followed in a substantial number of cases. "Last-hired, first-fired" policies were perceived by 61 percent of the respondents to have no impact and by 32 percent to have impeded productivity action. The high number of responses in the "no impact" category probably reflects the relatively few number of reductions in force related to the productivity actions selected.

Collective bargaining has also been largely covered in the discussion of imped-iments and likely impediments. The only factor not in one of these categories is the attitude of management toward productivity as a bargaining issue, which received a relatively even distribution of responses across the three categories.

Finally, the responses in the EEO-Affirmative Action section are notable for their concentration in the "no impact" category.

In addition to determining what the impact of various components of personnel management had been on the implementation of productivity actions, it is also important to ascertain in which areas the potential for improvement lies. Tables B-5 and B-6 report in tabular form the responses to questions about potential impacts. Table B-5 reports the responses to a yes/no question as to whether the various factors could have provided greater support to the productivity actions. Table B-6 reports the responses of a follow-up question which asked those respondents who had indicated that more than one factor within a component of personnel management could have helped to indicate which of those factors could have helped most. The distribution of responses is discussed in the last portion of chapter 2.

The final section of the survey response to be reported is from question 2 of the introductory section of the questionnaire. Here the respondents were asked to assess the impact of various laws, city offices, and groups on the imple-mentation of productivity actions in their cities. Several interesting patterns emerge from the distributions reported in Table B-7.

The city manager/chief executive was viewed as the most helpful in the implementation of productivity actions, significantly more so than all other offices, groups, or laws, with the possible exception of line department heads. The city budget office was next in the ranking, while the mayors' office, city council, and personnel office received substantially less support. These patterns are quite consistent with prior expectations regarding the impact of these offices on productivity actions. It seems that most of the productivity actions which are implemented are those which the chief executive officer, whether city manager or mayor, chooses to push. The very high rating accorded to the efforts of department heads should be interpreted as emphasizing the important role of the department heads in the conduct of the cities' day-to-day business. The similarly high rating given the budget offices seems consistent with their role in analysis and evaluation of programs. The somewhat higher number of times the budget office was viewed as impeding productivity actions probably reflects differences of opinion as to whether a productivity action actually was likely to improve effectiveness or efficiency. The lower rating accorded to the personnel office and the city councils is consistent with a role of facilitation and approval of the productivity actions rather than the initiation and imple-mentation of such activities.

Views on those factors which did not facilitate the implementation of productivity actions are just as interesting as those just discussed. Citizen groups

Table B-5
Which Factors Could Have Provided Greater Support for Productivity Actions?

	Could Have Provided Greater Support	Could Not Have
Recruitment and Selection:		
Procedures for recruiting personnel	62.5%	37.5%
Qualifications of candidates produced by the recruiting efforts	65.6	34.4
Selection standards, in relation to the qualifications required by productivity actions	63.3	36.7
Selection devices/tests and procedures	65.7	34.3
"Rule of three" or other similar selection rules	51.7	48.3
Procedures for processing candidates for appointment	50.2	49.8
Average	59.8	40.2
Classification:		
Classification standards (the established criteria for use in classifying positions)	66.9	31.1
Class specifications (the stated characteristics and qualifications requirements of groups of similar positions)	63.3	36.7
Position descriptions (written in standard form and language)	58.2	41.9
Procedures for getting positions classified properly	76.4	23.5
Average	66.2	33.8
Compensation:		
Salaries and benefits as compared with those of private industry and public employers	59.4	40.6
Relationship of pay levels to the quantity, quality, and degree of difficulty of employees' outputs	74.0	26.0
Procedures for establishing or changing pay levels	65.7	34.2
Procedures for establishing or changing fringe benefits	48.5	51.5
Policies and procedures for rewarding superior performance (through increased pay or benefits)	79.3	20.7
Average	65.4	34.6
Performance Appraisal:		
Coverage of the employee performance appraisal system (i.e., proportion of employees' included)	45.3	54.7

Table B-5 (Continued)

	Could Have Provided Greater Support	Could Not Have
Performance Appraisal: (Continued)		
Procedures for evaluating employees' performance	62.9%	37.2%
Policies or standards for identifying inadequate, acceptable, and superior performance	73.8	26.2
Established methods of evaluating performance	63.9	36.1
Average	61.5	38.5
Employee Development:		
Coverage of formal employee development plan (i.e., proportion of employees included in a plan that identifies the specific training or developmental needs of employees)	70.0	30.0
Procedures for identifying training needs	76.5	23.5
Policies and procedures for obtaining training or developmental assignments for employees	70.0	30.0
Policies and procedures for including training requirements in the planning for productivity-related actions	80.0	20.0
Encouragements (such as liberal leave policies and tuition payments) for employees to obtain outside training or education	53.1	46.9
Procedures for matching training to the actual needs of employees	77.7	22.3
Average	71.2	28.8
Promotion, Transfer, and Termination:		
Policies on considering employee performance in promotions and key lateral transfers	77.6	22.4
Policies on considering seniority in promotions and key lateral transfers	29.6	70.4
Time-in-grade (or similar) requirements for employees to be considered for promotions	26.1	73.9
Policies and procedures for terminating employees "for cause"	63.4	36.6
"last-hired, first-fired" (or similar) policies on terminations of employees during reductions-in-force	24.6	75.4
Procedures for processing promotion, transfer, and termination actions	59.2	40.9
Average	46.8	53.2

Table B-5 (Continued)

	Could Have Provided Greater Support	Could Not Have
Employee-Employer Relations:		
Established procedure for management consultation with employees in the planning, development, and implementation of productivity actions	73.8	26.2
Provisions for direct participation by employee representatives in the planning, development, and implementation of productivity actions	73.8	26.2
Employee attitude toward consulting with management on planning, developing, or implementing productivity actions	75.4	24.5
Management attitude toward consulting with employees on planning, developing, or implementing productivity actions	73.3	26.7
Average	74.1	25.9
Collective Bargaining:		
Labor-management agreement provisions relating to worker productivity	71.1	28.9
Number of separate bargaining units	39.7	60.2
Attitude of unions or employee organizations toward productivity as a bargaining issue	80.2	19.8
Attitude of management toward productivity as a bargaining issue	62.2	37.8
Procedures for the bargaining process	53.4	46.6
Grievance procedures	41.7	58.3
Average	58.1	41.9
EEO-Affirmative Action:		
EEO antidiscrimination policies and procedures	41.2	58.7
Affirmative Action guidelines	40.5	59.5
Hiring and/or promotion quotas	27.5	72.5
EEO-Affirmative Action appeal or complaint procedures	41.3	58.7
Average	37.6	62.4

Note: This table was compiled from question 3 of the questionnaire. Percentages are weighted averages in which each individual response is weighted in inverse proportion to the total number of responses from that city. "Don't Know" answers are not included.

Table B-6
Which Factors Could have Provided the Greatest Support for Productivity Actions?

Recruitment and Selection:

Procedures for recruiting personnel	18.1%
Qualifications of candidates produced by the recruiting efforts	19.4
Selection standards, in relation to the qualifications required by productivity actions	18.1
Selection devices/tests and procedures	25.0
"Rule of three" or other similar selection rules	9.7
Procedures for processing candidates for appointment	6.9
Other	2.8
Total	100.0

Classification:

Classification standards (the established criteria for use in classifying positions)	23.9
Class specifications (the stated characteristics and qualifications requirements of groups of similar positions)	16.4
Position descriptions (written in standard form and language)	14.9
Procedures for getting positions classified properly	40.3
Other	4.5
Total	100.0

Compensation:

Salaries and benefits as compared with those of private industry and public employers	12.3
Relationship of pay levels to the quantity, quality, and degree of difficulty of employees' outputs	20.2
Procedures for establishing or changing pay levels	11.2
Procedures for establishing or changing fringe benefits	2.2
Policies and procedures for rewarding superior performance (through increased pay or benefits)	53.9
Total	99.8

Performance and Appraisal:

Coverage of the employee performance appraisal system (i.e., proportion of employees included)	7.1
Procedures for evaluating employees' performance	14.3
Policies or standards for identifying inadequate, acceptable, and superior performance	55.4
Established methods of evaluating performance	19.6
Other	3.6
Total	100.0

Table B-6 (Continued)

Employee Development:

Coverage of formal employee development plan (i.e., proportion of employees included in a plan that identifies the specific training or developmental needs of employees)	17.0%
Procedures for identifying training needs	17.0
Policies and procedures for obtaining training or developmental assignments for employees	10.6
Policies or procedures for including training requirements in the planning for productivity-related actions	12.8
Encouragements (such as liberal leave policies and tuition payments) for employees to obtain outside training or education	11.7
Procedures for matching training to the actual needs of employees	29.8
Other	1.1
Total	100.0

Promotions, Transfers, and Terminations:

Policies on considering employee performance in promotions and key lateral transfers	41.1
Policies on considering seniority in promotions and key lateral transfers	5.5
Time-in-grade (or similar) requirements for employees to be considered for promotions	4.1
Policies and procedures for terminating employees "for cause"	23.3
"last-hired, first-fired" (or similar) policies on terminations of employees during reductions-in-force	1.4
Procedures for processing promotion, transfer, and termination actions	23.3
Other	1.4
Total	100.1

Employee-Employer Relations:

Established procedure for management consultation with employees in the planning, development, and implementation of productivity actions	23.3
Provisions for direct participation by employee representatives in the planning, developing, and implementation of productivity actions	29.1
Employee attitude toward consulting with management on planning, developing, or implementing productivity actions	17.4
Management attitude toward consulting with employees on planning, developing, or implementing productivity actions	30.2
Total	100.0

Collective Bargaining:

Labor-management agreement provisions relating to worker productivity	36.5%
Number of separate bargaining units	7.7
Attitude of unions or employee organizations toward productivity as a bargaining issue	25.0
Attitude of management toward productivity as a bargaining issue	13.5
Procedures for the bargaining process	11.5
Grievance procedures	5.8
Total	100.0

Table B-6 (Continued)

EEO-Affirmative Action:

EEO antidiscrimination policies and procedures	34.5%
Affirmation Action guidelines	24.1
Hiring and/or promotion quotas	20.7
EEO-Affirmative Action appeal or complaint procedures	17.2
Other	3.4
Total	99.9

Note: This table was compiled from those responses to question 3 of the questionnaire in which more than one of the factors within a component was judged capable of greater support for productivity actions. Of the two or more factors indicated, the respondent was asked to choose that which had the greatest potential. Percentages are weighted averages in which each individual response is weighted in inverse proportion to the total number of responses from that city. Those respondents who indicated only one factor (or none) within a component of personnel management could have provided greater support for productivity actions were not included. Due to rounding, totals may not equal 100.0 percent.

Table B-7
Impact of City Offices, Groups, and Laws on Productivity Actions

	Impeded	No Impact	Helped
Mayor's Office	2.8	41.0	56.2
City council	14.4	17.3	68.3
City manager/chief administrator	6.7	7.6	85.7
City budget office	10.3	10.3	79.4
Personnel office	18.1	18.2	63.7
Department heads	6.6	9.3	84.2
Employee organizations or unions	42.0	34.0	24.0
Citizen groups	23.9	47.4	28.7
Federal laws	53.1	28.5	15.4
State laws	50.0	30.0	20.0
City laws	29.3	34.0	36.6
Aggregate average	23.4	25.2	51.1

Note: Mayor's office includes only results for six of the eight cities. In the other two, St. Paul and Nashville, the mayor is the chief executive and more similar to the city manager.

and city laws or regulations were viewed as having a net effect of "no impact" on the cities' productivity actions. The lack of impact of city laws or regulations probably reflects the fact that if the city council desires to implement a particular productivity action which conflicts with local statutes or regulations, they have the power to change the law. The distribution of responses on citizen groups is concentrated around the "no impact" category. This probably reflects the fact that citizen groups tend to organize around narrower issues, such as the delivery of a particular service. Thus the support or opposition of citizen groups to a particular project probably hinges more on the impact of that project on total output of that service rather than the efficiency of the service.

In contrast to the views of the two preceding categories, federal laws and regulations, state laws and regulations, and employee organizations or unions all were seen as having significantly impeded the implementation of productivity actions. The state and federal laws are beyond the control of the local governments and apparently they do impinge upon managerial flexibility. An interesting sidelight is that the respondents from the South (Scottsdale, Savannah, Nashville) seemed to view the federal government regulations as more restrictive than state laws and regulations, while the opposite seemed to be true of the respondents from the North (all others, except Lakewood). This may reflect geographical differences in state laws covering public-sector collective bargaining. This interpretation also would be consistent with the negative impact employee organizations apparently have on the implementation of productivity actions.

Sample Respondents

The results reported in this appendix and in chapter 2 of this book are based on the responses of 169 individuals in eight cities. The number of responses did vary between cities, principally because of variations in the size and organization of the city governments involved. The primary selection criterion was to include all the city managerial employees who would be likely to have sufficiently broad knowledge of the city government to be reasonably familiar with the subject of the questionnaires. Approximately 20 percent of the respondents were from the personnel departments of the eight cities, 22 percent were from budget and productivity offices, and 37 percent of the respondents were from line departments. The remaining 21 percent of the respondents were from the city managers'/mayors' offices and city legislatures.

Because of the differences between cities in the number of respondents, all the responses have been weighted in the tabulations. The weighting factors were designed to attribute equal weights to the eight cities rather than equal weights to each of the questionnaires. This was accomplished by multiplying each response by a weighting factor proportional to the inverse of the number of completed questionnaires in each city. Table B-8 presents the distribution of the number of completed questionnaires by city and the weighting factors used.

A final piece of information about the responses to the survey relates to the number of "don't know" answers. Every question in the survey instrument allowed respondents to indicate "don't know," and respondents were encouraged to use that response if in fact they did not know. A considerable number of responses were anticipated in this category because of the diversity across the eight cities and the productivity actions.

The percentages of "don't know" responses for components of personnel management are reported in table B-9. The percentages reported in table B-9 are the percent of the total responses to questions relating specific factors within

Table B-8
The Distribution of Responses and Weighting Factors Across Cities

City	The Number Completed Questionnaires	Weighting Factor
Lakewood	18	.9444
Scottsdale	21	.8095
Tacoma	41	.4146
Worcester	17	1
Savannah	22	.7727
St. Paul	24	.7083
Dayton	21	.8095
Nashville	25	.6800

Note: The weighting factor was computed by the formula $WF = N_s/N_i$, where N_s is the smallest number of completed questionnaires in a city (17 in Worcester) and N_i is the number of completed questionnaires in a particular city.

Table B-9
The Percentage of "Don't Know" Responses for the Nine Personnel Management Components.

Recruitment and selection	36.9%
Classification	26.0
Compensation	20.4
Performance appraisal	32.8
Employee development	25.9
Promotions, transfers, and terminations	28.9
Employee-employer relations	24.8
Collective bargaining	49.2
EEO-Affirmative Action	42.5
Average	32.4

Note: Percentages are weighted averages across cities. See text for a description of the categories included.

the nine components of personnel management to the general concept of productivity improvement which were in the "don't know" category. Examination of these percentages reveals that there is indeed a substantial portion of the responses in the "don't know" category, but also that the portion in this category is not so large as to be alarming. The "don't know" responses are fairly evenly spread among the eight cities, except for collective bargaining questions. With the exceptions of collective bargaining, EEO-Affirmative Action, and recruitment and selection, they are evenly spread across the components of personnel management. The high percentage on collective bargaining is at least partly due to the relative lack of collective bargaining in Nashville, Savannah, and Lakewood, while the high percentage of EEO-Affirmative Action is probabaly explained by the general lack of impact of EEO-Affirmative Action on productivity action in these cities.

The percentage of responses in the "don't know" category is somewhat reassuring. It indicates that the respondents were willing to admit their lack of knowledge about particular components of personnel management or about specific productivity actions. This level of admitted lack of knowledge seems reasonable given the very specific productivity actions and the specificity of the factors within each of the components of personnel management. However, the percentages indicate that the sample of respondents on any particular question averages 140 respondents in the compensation section; approximately 130 respondents in the classification, employee development, and employee-employer relations sections; 120 in promotions, transfers, and terminations; 115 in performance appraisal; and 107 in recruitment and selection. These sample sizes seem quite adequate to justify confidence in the findings.

Bibliography

Aiken, M., and J. Hage. "The organic organization and innovation." *Sociology* 5:63-82, 1971.

Aplin, J.C., Jr., and P.P. Schoderbek. "How to measure management by objectives." *Public Personnel Management* 5(2):88, March-April 1976.

Auletta, K. "More for less." *The New Yorker*, August 1, 1977, pp. 30-48.

Bach, H. "The merit track in local government: Abused and diffused." *Public Personnel Management* 5(2):116, March-April 1976.

Balk, W.L., Symposium Editor. "Symposium on productivity in government." *Public Administration Review* 38(1):1-50, January-February 1978.

Balk, W.L. "Technological trends in productivity measurement." *Public Personnel Management* 5(2):128, March-April 1975.

Becker, H.M. "Sociometric location and innovativeness: Reformulation and extension of the diffusion model." *American Sociological Review* 35:267-282, 1970.

Beckman, N., Symposium Editor. "Symposium on policy analysis in government: Alternatives to 'muddling through.'" *Public Administration Review* 37(3):221-263, May-June 1977.

Beer, M., and R.A. Ruh. "Employee growth through performance management." *Harvard Business Review* 54(4):59, July-August 1976.

Bingham, R.D. *Innovation, bureaucracy, and public policy: A study of innovation adoption by local government.* Milwaukee, Wis.: Univ. of Wisconsin, Urban Research Center, 1976.

Bower, J.L. "Effective public management: It isn't the same as effective business management." *Harvard Business Review* 55(2):131-140, March-April 1977.

Broedling, L.A. "The uses of intrinsic-extrinsic distinction in explaining motivation and organizational behavior." *Academy of Management Review* 2:267-276, April 1977.

Calhoun, R., and T.H. Judee. "First level supervisory training and needs and organizational development." *Public Personnel Management* 4(3):196, May-June 1975.

Carter, S. "Trends in local government productivity." In *Municipal Year Book.* Washington, D.C.: International City Management Association, 1975, pp. 180-184.

Center for Productive Public Management. *Public Productivity Review.* New York, New York: John Jay College of Criminal Justice, City University of New York, 1976.

Cole, J.D.R., and A.S. Udler. "Productivity and personnel." *Civil Service Journal* 17(2):23, October-December 1976.

Committee for Economic Development, Research and Policy Committee. *Improving Productivity in State and Local Government.* New York, N.Y.: Committee for Economic Development, March 1976.

Courturier, J.J., and S.E. Dunn. "Federal colonization of state and local governments: The private parts of the public service." Paper prepared for the 1976 Conference of the American Society of Public Administration, Washington, D.C., April 1976.

Craver, G. "Survey of job evaluation practices in state and county governments." *Public Personnel Management* 5(2):121, March-April 1976.

Dahl, R. *Who Governs?* New Haven, Conn.: Yale Univ. Press, 1961.

Dallas, J. "Making the contract work at the local level." *Public Personnel Management* 6(5):320, September-October 1977.

Downey, E.H., and W. Balk. *Employee Innovation and Government Productivity: A Study of Suggestion Systems in the Public Sector.* Chicago, Ill.: International Personnel Management Association, 1976.

Downs, G.W., and L.B. Mohr. "Conceptual issues in the study of innovation." Paper presented to the annual meeting of the American Political Science Association, San Francisco, 1975.

Drucker, P.F. "Managing the public service institution." *The Public Interest*: 43-60, 1974.

_____. "New templates for today's organizations." *Harvard Business Review* 52(1):45-53, January-February 1974.

Feller, I., D. Menzel, and L. Kozak. "The diffusion of innovation in municipal governments." Final report to the National Science Foundation.

Fields, H.S., and W. Holley. "Traits in performance ratings: Their importance in public employment." *Public Personnel Management* 4(5):327, September-October 1975.

Finkle, A. "Governmental economic intervention and the merit system." *Public Personnel Management* 5(2):78, March-April 1976.

First Western Conference on Municipal Productivity and Quality of Working Life. "Partners for Productivity." *Public Productivity Review* 1:4-22, Summer 1976.

Flax, M.J. *A Study in Comparative Urban Indicators: Conditions in 18 Large Metropolitan Areas*, 1206-4. Washington, D.C.: The Urban Institute, April 1972.

Ford, R.C., and K. Jennings. "How to make performance appraisals more effective." *Personnel* 54:51-56, March-April 1977.

Foulkes, F.R. "The expanding role of the personnel function." *Harvard Business Review* 53(2):71, March-April 1975.

Foulkes, F., and H.M. Morgan. "Organizing and staffing the personnel function." *Harvard Business Review* 55(3):102, May-June 1977.

Foy, N. "Action learning comes to industry." *Harvard Business Review* 55(5):158-168, September-October 1977.

Garn, H.A., et al. *Models for Indicator Development: A Framework for Policy Analysis.* Washington, D.C.: The Urban Institute, 1976.

Gibson, R.E. *Increasing Employee Productivity.* New York, N.Y.: AMACOM. 1976.

Giegold, W.D., and R.J. Dunsing. "Team-building in the local jurisdiction: Two case studies." *Public Administration Review* 38(1):59-63, January-February 1978.

Goodman, C.F. "Judicial trends in public personnel management." *Public Personnel Management* 4(5):278, September-October 1975.

Gray, V. "Innovation in the states: A diffusion study." *American Political Science Review* 67:1171-1185, 1973.

Greer, A.L. "Advances in the study of diffusion of innovation in health care organizations." *Milbank Memorial Fund Quarterly* (forthcoming).

Greiner, J.M., R.E. Dahl, H.P. Hatry, and A.P. Millar. *Monetary Incentives and Work Standards in Five Cities: Impacts and Implications for Management and Labor*. Washington, D.C.: The Urban Institute, 1977.

Hackman, J.R. "Is job enrichment just a fad?" *Harvard Business Review* 53(5): 129, September-October 1975.

Haggerty, P.E. *The Productive Society*. New York, N.Y.: Carnegie-Mellon University, 1974.

Hatry, H.P., and D.M. Fisk. *Improving Productivity and Productivity Measurement in Local Governments*. Washington, D.C.: The Urban Institute for the National Commission on Productivity, June 1971.

Hayes, F. O'R. *Productivity in Local Government*. Lexington, Mass.: Lexington Books, 1977.

Hayward, N.S. "The productivity challenge." *Public Administration Review* 36(5):544-550, September-October 1976.

Heisel, W.D. "A new try at performance evaluation." *Agency Issues, International Personnel Management*:4-6, September 1977.

Hellwig, K.D. "Ten steps toward successful work measurement." *Management World* 5:3-6, November 1976.

Herrick, N.Q. *The Quality of Work and Its Outcomes: Estimating Potential Increases in Labor Productivity*. Columbus, Ohio: Academy for Contemporary Problems, September 1975.

Herzberg, F. "Motivation, job enrichment and productivity." *Bulletin on Training* 2:1-4, May-June 1977.

Herzberg, F., B. Mausner, and B. Snyderman. *The Motivation to Work*. New York, N.Y.: Wiley, 1959.

Hill, N.C. "The effect of self-esteem on productivity improvement." *Supervisor* 39:2-3, March 1977.

Horton, R.D. "Productivity and productivity bargaining in government: A critical analysis." *Public Administration Review* 36(4):407-414, July-August 1976.

Howe, R.J. "Building teams for increased productivity." *Personnel Journal* 56:16-22, January 1977.

Husel, W.D. "The personnel revolution: An optimist's view." *Public Personnel Management* 5(4):234, July-August 1976.

Imundo, L.V., Jr. "Ineffectiveness and inefficiency in government management." *Public Personnel Management* 4(2):90, March-April 1975.

International City Management Association. *The Municipal Yearbook 1976.* Washington, D.C., 1976.

Jacobs, A.A. "What's wrong with performance evaluation programs?" *Supervisory Management* 22:10-15, July 1977.

Jaccbs, R., and T. Solomon. "Strategies for enhancing the prediction of job performance from job satisfaction." *Journal of Applied Psychology* 62(4):417-421, August 1977.

Janka, K.C., et al. *People, Performance. . .Results: A Guide to Increasing the Effectiveness of Local Government Employees.* Washington, D.C.: National Training and Development Service Press, 1977.

Jones, R.T. *Public Sector Labor Relations: An Evaluation of Policy-Related Research.* Belmont, Mass.: Contract Research Corporation, February 1975.

Katzell, R.A., et al. *Work, Productivity, and Job Satisfaction: An Evaluation of Policy-Related Research.* New York, N.Y.: The Psychological Corporation, January 1975.

Kempe, R. "Merit promotion and equal employment opportunity." *General Accounting Office Review* 11:80-82, Winter 1977.

Knowles, M.S. "Human resources development in OD." *Public Administration Review* 34(2):115-123, March-April 1974.

Kraemer, K.L. "Local government information systems and technology transfer: Evaluating some common assertions about computer application transfer." *Public Administration Review* 37(4):368-382, July-August 1977.

Lee, R.D., Jr., and W. Juleanovic. "Personnel management information systems for state and local governments." *Public Personnel Management* 4(2):84, March-April 1975.

Lefaver, S., and R. Jaeck. "Compensation for public managers: A different way." *Public Personnel Management* 6(4):269, July-August 1977.

Levinson, H. "Appraisal of what performance? (Thinking ahead)." *Harvard Business Review* 54(4):30, July-August 1976.

Levinson, P., and M. Sugar. "Performance evaluation and rating." *Civil Service Journal* 18(1); July-September 1977.

Lewin, D. "Aspects of wage determination in local government employment." *Public Administration Review* 34(2):149-155, March-April 1974.

————. "The prevailing wage principle and public wage decisions." *Public Personnel Management* 3(6); November-December 1974.

The LGMP Team. *The LGMP Experience: Guidelines for Organizational Change in Local Government.* Kingston, Canada: Queen's University School of Business, Local Government Management Project, April 1977.

Lyden, F.J., Editor. "Productivity management: A multifaceted learning package." *Public Administration Review* 34(2):163-164, March-April 1974.

Mansfield, E. "Speed of response of firms in new techniques." *Quarterly Journal of Economics* 77:290-311, 1973.

Maslow, A.H. *Motivation and Personality.* New York, N.Y.: Harper and Brothers, 1954.

McAfee, B., and B. Green. "Selecting a performance appraisal method." *Personnel Administrator* 22:61-64, June 1977.

McDermott, F.A. "Merit systems under fire." *Public Personnel Management* 5(4):225, July-August 1976.

McIntyre, D.I. "Merit principles and collective bargaining: A marriage or divorce." *Public Administration Review* 37(2):186-190, March-April 1977.

McKenna, H. "Managing change in government." *Civil Service Journal* 17(4):1, April-June 1977.

Merrill, P., and T.K. Kumar. *Productivity Management in Administrative Services: Budgeting and Management Analysis in Public Service Institutions,* Report no. AAI-77-56. Cambridge, Mass.: Abt Associates, Inc., June 1977.

Merton, R.K. *Social Theory and Social Structure.* New York, N.Y.: Free Press, 1949.

Meyer, H.E. "Personnel directors are the new corporate heroes." *Fortune*:84-88, February 1976.

Meyer, M., and W. Williams, "Comparison of innovation in public and private sectors. An exploratory study." Report to NSF. Riverside California: Univ. of California. 1976.

Mills, T. "Human resources—Why the new concern?" *Harvard Business Review* 53(2):120-134, March-April 1975.

Mohr, L.B. "Determinants of innovation in organizations." *American Political Science Review* 63:111-126, 1969.

Mondello, A.L. "Management excellence and public policies." *Civil Service Journal* 16(2):17, October-December 1975.

Moore, P. "Rewards and public employees' attitudes toward client service." *Public Personnel Management* 6:98-105, March-April 1977.

Mushkin, S.J. *Staffing Services to People in the Cities. No. 9. Do Productivity Measures Pay Off for Employee Performance?* Washington, D.C.: Public Services Laboratory, Georgetown University, 1975.

Mushkin, S.J., and F.H. Sandifer. "Productivity in tax administration: Personnel management factors." In *Public Personnel Administration; Policies and Practices for Personnel,* Report Bulletin 6, Vol. 5. Englewood Cliffs, N.J.: Prentice-Hall, September 20, 1977, pp. 531-533.

Mushkin, S.J., F.H. Sandifer, and C. Warren. *Assessing Personnel Management: Objectives and Performance Indicators.* Washington, D.C.: Public Services Laboratory, Georgetown University, March 1977.

Mustafa, H., and R.D. Sylvia. "A factor-analysis approach to job satisfaction." *Public Personnel Management* 4(3):165, May-June 1975.

Myers, S. "Conditions for manager motivation." *Harvard Business Review* 44(1):58-71, January -February 1966.

Nassau County, New York, Multi-Municipal Productivity Project. *An Approach to Productivity Improvement in the Public Sector.* Springfield, Virginia: National Technical Information Service, 1975.

National Civil Service League. *Model Public Personnel Administration Law.* Washington, D.C.: National Civil Service League, November 1970.

National Commission on Productivity. *Labor-Management Committees in the Public Sector: Experience of Eight Communities.* Washington, D.C.: National Commission on Productivity, 1975.

_____. *So, Mr. Mayor, You Want to Improve Productivity.* Washington, D.C.: National Commission on Productivity, 1974.

National Commission on Productivity and Work Quality. *Employee Incentives to Improve State and Local Government Productivity.* Washington, D.C.: U.S. Government Printing Office, March 1975.

_____. *Improving Municipal Productivity: Work Measurement for Better Management.* Washington, D.C.: U.S. Government Printing Office. 1975.

_____. *Jurisdictional Guide to Public Sector Productivity Improvement Projects.* Washington, D.C.: National Commission on Productivity and Work Quality, 1976.

_____. *Managing Human Resources in Local Government: A Survey of Employee Incentive Plans.* Washington, D.C.: The Urban Institute, October 1973.

The National League of Cities, Office of Policy Analysis and Development. *State of the Cities: 1975, A New Urban Crisis?* Washington, D.C.: The National League of Cities, January 1976.

National Science Foundation. *Research on Productivity Measurement Systems for Administrative Services,* NSF Program Announcement No. 75-14. Washington, D.C.: National Science Foundation, Division of Advanced Productivity Research and Technology, 1975.

New York City Productivity Council. *Improving Productivity in Municipal Agencies: A Labor-Management Approach.* New York, N.Y.: New York City Productivity Council, October 1975.

Newland, C.A. "Public personnel administration: Legalistic reforms vs. effectiveness, efficiency, and economy." *Public Administration Review* 36(5): 529-537, September-October 1976.

Newstrom, J.W., W.E. Reif, and R.M. Monczka. "Motivating the public employee: Fact vs. fiction." *Public Personnel Management* 5:67-72, January-February 1976.

Nininger, J.R. and V.N. MacDonald. *The LGMP Experience: Phase I. Assessing Readiness for Organizational Change in Local Government. Kingston, Canada: Queen's University School of Business, Local Government Management Project, January 1977.*

Nollen, S.D. *The Effect of Collective Bargaining on Municipal Personnel Systems: A Research Review.* Washington, D.C.: Public Services Laboratory, Georgetown University, 1975.

Olmer, R.E. "The operating personnel office: A working dichotomy." *Civil Service Journal* 18(2):30, October-December 1977.

Pajer, R. *Job Analysis for Improved Job Related Selection.* Washington, D.C.: U.S. Civil Service Commission, 1976.

Paly, A.L. "Performance appraisal: Useful but still resisted." *Harvard Business Review* 53(3):74, May-June 1975.

Panel of the National Academy of Public Administration. *Improving Personnel Management in State and Local Government: A Review of the Grants Program of the Intergovernmental Personnel Act*. Washington, D.C.: National Academy of Public Administration, March 1976.

Pathak, D.S., G. Burton, and R. Zigli. "A comparative study of work incentives for professional employees." *Michigan Business Review* 29:27-32, July 1977.

Perkins, R. *Evaluating Service Productivity and Efficiency: A Bibliography*. Honolulu, Hawaii: Honolulu Municipal References and Records Center, 1976.

Persson, L.N. "A method for determining what the job is worth." *Administration and Management* 37:57-58, March 1977.

Pinder, C. "Concerning the application of human motivation theories in organizational settings." *Academy of Management Review* 2:384-397, July 1977.

Pizam, A. "Social differentiation: A new psychological barrier to performance appraisal." *Public Personnel Management* 4(4):244, July-August 1975.

Public Services Laboratory. *Staffing Services to People in the Cities: A Series of Research Reviews*, Numbers 1-10. Washington, D.C.: Public Services Laboratory, Georgetown University, 1975.

Ramsay, A.S. "The new factor evaluation system of position classification." *Civil Service Journal* 16(3):15, January-March 1976.

Rapp, B.W., F.M. Patitucci. *Managing Local Government for Improved Performance: A Practical Approach*. Boulder, Colorado: Westview Press, 1977.

Rich, W.C., Symposium Editor. "Mini-symposium on the municipal service under pressure" *Public Administration Review* 37(5):505-519, September-October 1977.

Roessner, J.D. "Federal policy and the application of technology to state and local government problems." *Policy Analysis* (forthcoming).

Rogers, E.M. *Diffusion of Innovations*. New York, N.Y.: Free Press, 1962.

Rogers, E.M., and F.F. Shoemaker. *Communication of Innovations: A Cross-Cultural Approach*. New York, N.Y.: Free Press, 1971.

Rosen, B. *The Merit System in the United States Civil Service*. A monograph prepared for the Committee on Post Office and Civil Service, U.S. House of Representatives, 94th Congress, 1st Session. Washington, D.C.: U.S. Government Printing Office, December 23, 1975.

——. "Partners in productivity." *Civil Service Journal* 15 (3):16, January-March 1975.

Rosow, J.M. "Public sector pay and benefits." *Public Administration Review* 36 (5):538-543, September-October 1976.

Rosow, J.M., Editor. *The Worker and the Job*. Englewood Cliffs, N.J.: Prentice-Hall, 1974.

Ross, J.P., and J. Burkhead. *Productivity in the Local Government Sector*. Lexington, Mass.: Lexington Books, 1974.

Salton, G.J. "Varimat: Variable format performance appraisal." *Personnel Administrator* 22:53-58, June 1977.

Savas, E.S., and S.G. Ginsburg, "The civil service: A meritless system." *Public Interest*:70-85, Summer 1973.

Schmidt, F., J. Hunter, and V. Urry. *Statistical Power in Criterion Related Validation Studies*. Washington, D.C.: U.S. Civil Service Commission, Personnel Research and Development Center, 1976.

Schneier, C.E. "Multiple rates groups and performance appraisal." *Public Personnel Management* 6(1):13-20, January-February 1977.

Shapek, R.A. "Federal influences in state and local personnel management: The system in transition." *Public Personnel Management* 5(1):41, January-February 1976.

Siegel, G. "The enlarged concept of productivity measurement in government: A review of some strategies." *Public Productivity Review* 2:37-59, Winter 1976.

Silberger, S. "The missing public-collective bargaining in public employment." *Public Personnel Management* 4(5):290-299, September-October 1975.

"Some Fresh Ideas for Boosting Workers' Output." *U.S. News and World Report* 81, November 29, 1976, pp. 83-84.

Srivasta, S., et al. *Productivity, Industrial Organization and Job Satisfaction: Policy Development and Implementation*. Cleveland, Ohio: Case Western Reserve University School of Management, July 1974.

Stanley, D.T. *Managing Local Government Under Union Pressure*. Washington, D.C.: The Brookings Institution, 1972.

_____. *Professional Personnel for the City of New York*. Washington, D.C.: The Brookings Institution, 1963.

Sugarman, J. "Improving management through reorganization." *Civil Service Journal* 18(2):1, October-December 1977.

"The Tightening Squeeze of White-Collar Pay." *Business Week*, September 12, 1977, pp. 82-94.

The Urban Institute and International City Management Association. *Measuring the Effectiveness of Basic Municipal Services*, Initial Report. Washington, D.C.: The Urban Institute and International City Management Association, February 1974.

The Urban Institute and the National Association of State Budget Offices. *The Status of Productivity Measurement in State Government: An Initial Examination*. Washington, D.C.: U.S. Government Printing Office, 1976.

U.S. Bureau of the Census. *Labor-Management Relations in State and Local Governments: 1975*, Series GSS No. 81. Washington, D.C.: U.S. Government Printing Office, February 1977.

U.S. Civil Service Commission, Bureau of Intergovernmental Personnel Programs. *Guide to a More Effective Public Service: The Legal Framework*, BIPP 152-43. Washington, D.C.: U.S. Government Printing Office, August 1974.

U.S. Civil Service Commission. *Improving Employee Performance and Organizational Effectiveness*. Washington, D.C.: U.S. Government Printing Office, 1976.

_____. *Labor-Management Relations in the Public Service*, Personnel Bibliography Series. Washington, D.C.: U.S. Government Printing Office (issued annually).

_____. *Performance Evaluation: Resource Application Packet*. Washington, D.C.: Bureau of Personnel Management Evaluation, Clearinghouse on Productivity and Organizational Effectiveness, 1976.

_____. *Personnel Management in State and Local Governments*, Personnel Bibliography Series. Washington, D.C.: U.S. Government Printing Office (issued annually).

U.S. Department of Health, Education and Welfare. *Work in America.* Cambridge, Mass.: M.I.T. Press, 1973.

U.S. General Accounting Office. *Evaluation and Analysis to Support Decision-Making*, PAD-76-9. Washington, D.C.: U.S. Government Printing Office, September 1, 1976.

U.S. House of Representatives, Committee on Post Office and Civil Service. *History of Civil Service Merit Systems of the United States and Selected Foreign Countries.* Washington, D.C.: U.S. Government Printing Office, December 31, 1976.

U.S. Joint Financial Management Improvement Program. *Productivity Programs in the Federal Government.* Washington, D.C.: U.S. Joint Financial Management Improvement Program, 1976.

U.S. National Center for Productivity and Quality of Working Life. *1976 Annual Report to the President and Congress.* Washington, D.C.: U.S. Government Printing Office, 1977.

U.S. Office of Management and Budget. *Strengthening Public Management in the Intergovernmental System.* Washington, D.C.: Study Committee on Policy Management Assistance, Executive Office of the President, 1975.

Uselaner, B.L. "Productivity measurement: A management tool." *General Accounting Office Review* 10:54-59, Fall 1976.

Van Maanen, J., P. Gregg, and R. Katz. *Work in the Public Sector.* Washington, D.C.: National Training and Development Service for State and Local Government, 1975.

Walker, J.L. "Comment: Problems in research on the diffusion of policy innovations." *American Political Science Review* 67:1186-1191, 1973.

_____. "The diffusion of innovation among the American states." *American Political Science Review* 63:880-889, 1969.

Weiss, C.H. *Evaluation Research: Methods of Assessing Program Effectiveness.* Englewood Cliffs, N.J.: Prentice-Hall, 1972.

Whalen, G., and R. Rubin. "Labor relations and affirmative action: A tug of war." *Public Personnel Management* 5(3):149, May-June 1976.

White, R. "Personnel, power, and productivity." *Public Personnel Management* 6(4):225, July-August 1977.

Wholey, J.S., et al. *Federal Evaluation Policy: Analyzing the Effects of Public Programs.* Washington, D.C.: The Urban Institute, 1970.

Williams, R., J. Walker, and C. Fletcher. "International review of staff appraisal practices: Current trends and issues." *Public Personnel Management* 6(1):5, January-February 1977.

Wise, C. "Productivity in personnel administration and public policy." In H.G. Frederickson and C. Wise, *Public Administration and Public Policy*. Lexington, Mass.: Lexington Books, 1977.

Zagoria, S., Editor. *Public Workers and Public Unions*. Englewood Cliffs, N.J.: Prentice-Hall, 1972.

Zaltman, G., R. Duncan, and J. Holbeck. *Innovation and Organizations*. New York, N.Y.: Wiley, 1973.

Index

About the Authors

Selma J. Mushkin is an internationally recognized, widely published economist, noted for her excellent work in such diverse fields as health economics, public finance, policy analysis, and education. She has had a distinguished career in both government and academia. She has been the director of Public Services Laboratory at Georgetown University since its establishment.

Frank H. Sandifer was project manager of the study from which this book developed. He is associate director of the Public Services Laboratory and has written on various public management topics. He has held positions in both the legislative and executive branches of the federal government.

The Public Services Laboratory (PSL) was established at Georgetown University in 1970 as a research and educational institute to conduct and promote analysis and evaluation of public policy and management issues. An important objective of PSL is to strengthen the ties between the students, faculty, and staff of Georgetown and other universities and the managers, policymakers, and staffs of government organizations, particularly at the state and local levels of government. PSL has a dual aim of conducting expert research that has practical applications for policymakers and managers and providing educational experiences and materials for students and scholars on analysis of public issues. Since its founding, PSL has been directed by Dr. Selma J. Mushkin, professor of economics at Georgetown University.